JUST WAR AND THE
RESPONSIBILITY TO PROTECT

ABOUT THE AUTHORS

Robin Dunford and **Michael Neu** are both members of the Centre for Applied Philosophy, Politics and Ethics at the University of Brighton. They teach on degrees in War; Philosophy, Politics and Ethics; and Globalisation. Neu's previous book, *Just Liberal Violence*, was published in 2017; Dunford's *The Politics of Transnational Peasant Struggle* was published in 2016.

JUST WAR AND THE RESPONSIBILITY TO PROTECT

A CRITIQUE

Robin Dunford and Michael Neu

ZED

Just War and the Responsibility to Protect: A Critique was first published in 2019 by Zed Books Ltd, The Foundry, 17 Oval Way, London SE11 5RR, UK.

www.zedbooks.net

Copyright © Robin Dunford and Michael Neu 2019

The right of Robin Dunford and Michael Neu to be identified as the authors of this work has been asserted by them in accordance with the Copyright, Designs and Patents Act, 1988

Typeset in Plantin and Kievit by Swales & Willis Ltd, Exeter, Devon
Index by Robin Dunford and Michael Neu
Cover design by Steve Leard
Printed and bound by CPI Group (UK)Ltd, Croydon, CR0 4YY

Cover photo © Tommy Trenchard, Panos Pictures

A catalogue record for this book is available from the British Library

ISBN 978-1-78699-151-5 hb
ISBN 978-1-78699-150-8 pb
ISBN 978-1-78699-152-2 pdf
ISBN 978-1-78699-153-9 epub
ISBN 978-1-78699-154-6 mobi

CONTENTS

ABBREVIATIONS

ICISS	International Commission on Intervention and State Sovereignty
NATO	North Atlantic Treaty Organization
R2P	Responsibility to Protect
SAP	Structural Adjustment Programme
UN	United Nations

ACKNOWLEDGEMENTS

We would like to express our gratitude to a number of friends and colleagues who have made important contributions to this book. In particular, we thank Bob Brecher and Vicky Margree for insightful comments. Vasilis Leontisis has always been there, and the prospect of him giving us the "sh*t of our lives" has always kept us motivated. We had valuable conversations with Cathy Bergin, Garrett Wallace Brown, Zeina Maasri, Mark McGovern, Paul Reynolds and James Souter. Our former student Rob Somerton-Jones also provided useful comments on our Libya chapter. Many other students and colleagues have asked some great questions in response to talks we gave on a number of occasions – beginning with a talk on "Just Killing Gone Wrong" in a lecture theatre packed with undergraduates a couple of years ago. It was around this time that we first spoke to Ken Barlow, who has been a friendly, understanding and supportive editor throughout. The Humanities Programme and the Centre for Applied Philosophy, Politics and Ethics has, as ever, been a supportive and stimulating environment in which to write a book. This is in many ways thanks to Paddy Maguire, who has been a fabulous Head of School and should never have been allowed to retire.

On a more personal note, we'd both like to thank our families. Michael has worked on this book with his family under more strain than any of us would have imagined just over a year ago, but it is well documented that we are not to be defeated. Robin would like to thank Annabel Wyatt in particular, whose love and support has been a blissful relief throughout.

P.S. *Ich würde Euch dieses Buch ja widmen, aber es passt einfach nicht zu Euch. Warten wir lieber aufs nächste: über die Freundschaft.*

INTRODUCTION

In January 2017, eastern Aleppo in Syria was under siege. President Bashar al-Assad's forces had blocked all exit routes from the area. Russian planes provided air support, bombing rebel areas and killing civilians in the process. Aid was blocked, leaving people in the city starving and dying. Rebel fighters would not let civilians leave, knowing that they could be used as a shield from the Syrian regime. Reports from the area suggested that mass human rights violations were committed on all sides. This was but the latest episode in a conflict that, at the time of writing, has cost at least 400,000 lives and displaced half of Syria's population.

Speaking to the United Kingdom (UK) House of Commons as the siege was unfolding, Conservative Member of Parliament George Osborne (in Wintour, 2016a) said that events in Aleppo were 'created by a vacuum, a vacuum of Western leadership, of American leadership, British leadership'. The events highlighted, he continued, 'the price of not intervening'. Osborne's speech is reflective of the broader way in which mass atrocity situations are framed in public discourse, contemporary just war thinking and the Responsibility to Protect (R2P) – the international commitment to prevent and respond to mass atrocities. It is a framing that imagines that crises like the one in eastern Aleppo simply crop up. The international community is *not* seen to be involved in the emergence of such crises. Or, when the involvement of international actors is recognised, focus tends to fall on "villainous" actors like Russia, Iran and transnational Islamist militias, who are considered to stoke the flames after crises emerge. The "good international citizens", previously un-involved, then face a choice: intervene, which is often a euphemism for dropping bombs and perhaps waging full-scale war; or "stand aside" and watch the crisis unfold.

This framing is distorting. It misses the way in which Western leadership, and the actions and omissions of the self-styled international community more broadly, are important factors in the emergence of such crises. Look across the border to Iraq to see the effects of Western leadership. Look a little further to Libya, where North Atlantic Treaty Organization (NATO) leadership has helped produce a failed state that has allowed weapons to spread across the region to fuel conflict in Mali and Syria. Or look again to Syria where WikiLeaks has revealed that, as part of a strategy of destabilising the country in the hope of ending Assad's rule, the USA have been stoking ethnic tensions since the middle of the first decade of the 21st century. Consider also the way in which militant Islamism and Islamophobia have entered a vicious dance, inciting one another in what sometimes seems like a continued ratcheting up of both. Or consider the role that leaders of the international community have played in supporting and arming Saudi Arabia, in full knowledge that the Saudi government is bombing civilians in Yemen. And this is before we get to the extensive role played by Russia and Iran in Syria. To say that crises across the world are created exclusively or solely by international actors would be mistaken and serve to erase the agency of local actors. But to say that crises emerge in the vacuum of international or Western leadership is patently false. Crises in the Middle East and North Africa, much like crises across the world, do not emerge in a vacuum. They have the mark of the international community as well as the mark of Western leadership all over them. Intervention is *already* occurring. And it contributes to the creation of the very crises to which just war thinking and the R2P respond.

Already existing intervention has implications both for how we think about preventing mass atrocities and for how we understand the legitimacy of responses, especially military ones. In terms of prevention, it shows that there is a much richer array of preventative measures than exists within the repertoire of just war thinking and the R2P. In terms of responding, recognising the way in which the international community helps create crises reveals that would-be interveners are bad international citizens who are not fit for the purpose of military intervention. When actors stoke conflict, maintain unfair trade relations, sell arms that facilitate oppression and refuse to take in refugees displaced from conflict, they are not fit for the purpose of protecting people through military means. By calling for actors that are already stoking conflict to engage also in military intervention, just war thinking and the R2P do not improve responses to mass atrocity crimes. Instead, they legitimise militarist activity under a veneer of morality.

Introducing our book

Our book makes four main arguments. In what follows, we introduce these arguments, giving an outline of each chapter in the process.

Bringing reality back in

Just war thinking and the R2P fail to look at the impact of the humanitarian wars that they sometimes recommend. To bring reality back in we start, in the first chapter, with an investigation of NATO's 2011 intervention in Libya. This intervention was authorised by the United Nations (UN) Security Council on the basis that Libya was failing to fulfil its responsibility to protect civilians. According to academic and policy supporters of the R2P, the Libya intervention is an example of the R2P working 'exactly as it was supposed to' (Evans, 2012). This intervention, however, led to civilian deaths, displacement, sexual violence, regional instability and mass human rights violations. Chapter 2 begins by asking why, despite the horrors of the intervention, advocates of the R2P claim that Libya was a 'triumph' (Thakur, 2013, 69). We diagnose this catastrophic misjudgement by highlighting the ways in which writing on the R2P deletes the reality of humanitarian war from the picture. It takes as its object of analysis not the material effects of intervention but the way in which the idea of a responsibility to protect is used in high-level UN meetings. This focus continues in analyses of the wider record of the R2P. Contrary to Alex Bellamy's (2015a) claim that the R2P is improving responses to mass atrocity crimes, we point out that it has coincided with an increase in violence and atrocity. Failure to focus on the reality of war is not only endemic in the R2P but also in contemporary just war thinking, where theorists discuss the ethics of war on the basis of fanciful and distorting thought experiments. When reality is brought back in, it becomes apparent that humanitarian wars are far from just, and that the R2P is failing to improve international attempts to prevent and respond to mass atrocity crimes.

Already existing intervention and atrocity

Chapter 3 argues that just war thinking and the R2P operate within narrow and distorting frameworks. Reflecting Osborne's comments on Syria, they imagine a world in which states exist in separation from one another, with mass atrocity situations emerging through the failure or barbarism of particular states. When mass atrocities start to emerge, the international community tends to be identified either as a saviour that takes action to fulfil its responsibility to protect or as a passive onlooker that manifestly fails to act upon its stated commitment to human rights and civilian protection. This means that just war thinking and the R2P are blind to the ways in which international actors are already intervening and ignorant of the changes to already existing intervention that are required in order to prevent the occurrence of mass atrocity crimes.

Chapter 4 brings back into the picture these already existing practices of intervention. It shows that they create a world in which atrocity takes place as a matter of routine. In the Rwandan genocide, 800,000 people died during 100 days of killing. In part as a result of already existing intervention, more people die from hunger alone *every* 100 days. This is but one aspect of an everyday atrocity that sees people killed through environmental destruction, poverty and a failure to address global health inequalities. Everyday atrocity and the already existing interventions that help create it also make the very humanitarian crises that the R2P is supposed to address more likely to occur. To break beyond the narrow and distorting gaze characteristic of analyses of atrocity, we outline five global injustices that also create and perpetuate conflict.[1] In each case we demonstrate how the actors that just war theorists and advocates of the R2P identify as legitimate saviours are simultaneously reproducing long-term dynamics of conflict. We focus on: global inequalities and poverty, which we flesh out with reference to genocide in Rwanda and conflict in the former Yugoslavia; environmental destruction, which we discuss with reference to ethnic cleansing in Darfur; land grabbing and the production of food insecurity, which we analyse with reference to conflict in sub-Saharan Africa; divide and rule policies working to stoke ethnic tension, which we examine in the context of genocide in Rwanda and civil war in Syria; and arms trading, which we highlight through a discussion of civil war in Libya and Yemen. Taken together, these examples show that intervention is occurring *all of the time*, and that those called upon to save strangers are *at the same time* agents of oppression, generating conditions that are not only violent but also conducive to the continued emergence of mass atrocities.

Already existing intervention has implications for just war and the R2P

Recognising already existing intervention opens up avenues for prevention that go far beyond the preventative toolbox currently imagined in the R2P. But this only scratches the surface of the vital implications of already existing intervention and everyday atrocity, which we explore further in Chapter 5. We argue that in light of their current harmful practices, already intervening states are not fit for the purpose of military intervention. This is because the moral character of these states has a decisive impact on the way in which their military interventions play out. Contrary to the claim that states involved in wrongdoing can legitimately engage in humanitarian military intervention provided they have the material capacity to "get the job done", we should expect military interventions performed by bad international citizens to follow the example of Libya in having inhumanitarian impacts and failing to protect. It is therefore a mistake to call on actors who are already doing harm to engage also in military interventions.

The R2P is a dangerous norm that is not fit for the purpose of preventing and responding to mass atrocities

In the face of our criticisms, one might ask what would be left if we were to abandon the R2P. Is it not the one norm we have that places limits on the barbaric acts that states are capable of committing against their own people? Does it not do something, however minimal, to encourage states to care about what happens beyond their borders and to not simply stand by when events like the Syrian civil war occur? Shouldn't we work with what is already there, calling for achievable reforms that will improve the R2P? This kind of argument is very common. We are often told that the R2P is the most we can hope for. We should therefore work with it, rather than undermine our only protection against a world in which states do nothing but act in their own interests (see, e.g., Bellamy, 2015a). Even critics tend to suggest that the R2P is 'insufficient' and 'incomplete' and thus requires additional elements (Brown and Bohm, 2016, 897), or that it needs to be made more robust in order to ensure that states *have to* act when atrocities happen. Throughout this book, we argue that this reformist approach to R2P is fundamentally misguided. Why should we hope at all for a framework that helped enable and legitimise the devastating intervention in Libya and has made no progress in preventing and responding to mass atrocities? Why should we hope for a framework that excludes from the picture the everyday atrocity of mass avoidable death? Why should we hope for a framework that fails to focus on already existing interventions that contribute to the creation of mass atrocities? What is more, as Chapter 5 makes clear, the R2P is not just limited, insufficient or lacking in "oomph". It is fundamentally dangerous. Rather than limit violence, it helps legitimise it by framing the violence of bad international citizens as just, "civilised" and heroic. We argue that such a framing cannot contribute towards the goal of ending humanitarian disasters and mass atrocities. What is required is a radical set of changes – changes that would not only have major implications for the everyday practices of the actors that intervene, but also for the thinking, writing and advocacy work of those who see in these agents the potential saviours of victims of atrocity crimes. Instead of providing legitimation for military intervention, scholars and activists must look beyond their narrow framework and consider what can be done to prevent conflict from continually occurring. They must insist that bad international citizens change their already existing practices of intervention and replace them with practices that are more conducive to the long-term avoidance of conflict and atrocity.

◆ ◆ ◆

One challenge we faced when writing this book was delineating its boundaries. Our arguments relate to justifications of military intervention under what is known as pillar three of the R2P and, more specifically, to justifications of humanitarian war *in this world and this political context*: a context in which already existing intervention fuels conflict and generates mass avoidable death. They also relate to the broader frameworks of just war thinking and the R2P – frameworks that serve to occlude such intervention whilst justifying war in abstraction from its devastating effects. Our arguments do not necessarily hold, however, for all of the practices – including practices of peacekeeping, conflict resolution and diplomacy – that are sometimes (albeit controversially) understood to fall under the R2P. We do not, for instance, engage in the kind of analysis that would be required in order to assess African Union peace operations or other regional efforts at building peace. Nor do we discuss diplomatic attempts to prevent or put an end to conflict. Our arguments relate to justifications of *military* intervention in contexts of already existing intervention; to the distorting manner in which just war thinking portrays war; and to the overall framework of – if not all actions that might be considered to take place under – the R2P. The context-specific nature of our arguments also means that they do not speak to violence in contexts such as anti-colonial war, where it is carried out by actors who are themselves facing severe and violent oppression.

Another challenge stemmed from our attempt to make an original academic contribution while also engaging a wider audience. By virtue of making the four arguments outlined above, this book contributes to scholarship on just war and the R2P, and will be of interest to critics and supporters alike. It also addresses students and the wider pubic. There are a number of accessible defences of just war and the R2P, to which our book offers a counterpoint. We hope that it will change the minds of anyone who supports humanitarian wars and the R2P – committed as they are to ending mass atrocities. Our goal is to persuade them to rethink their current justifications of war, and encourage them to fight for changes that will make positive steps towards a fairer, less militaristic and more peaceful world. Finally, we hope that our book is of interest to advocates of peace, who so often face questions about what they would and should do in situations that shock the conscience of humanity. To this end, our conclusions on Rwanda and Syria outline how we, on the basis of the arguments developed in this book, would respond to precisely those questions that often get asked by those seeking legitimacy and authorisation for military intervention. If our book goes even a small way to supporting the case for a more peaceful and less militaristic world, it will have served its purpose.

Introducing just war

With our diverse intended audience in mind, the remainder of this introduction outlines the basic contours of just war and the R2P. If you, the reader, are already intimately familiar with these, you may want to go straight to Chapter 1.

The long tradition of just war, while not a unified body of thought, has principally been concerned with the question of when it is right to wage war.[2] But also when it is wrong. Leading contemporary just war theorist Michael Walzer (2004, 22), for example, insists on the tradition's critical edge, arguing that it 'makes actions and operations that are morally problematic *possible* by constraining their occasions and regulating their conduct'. War can be just only if (i) it has a just cause (i.e., the war is waged, for example, to resist aggression, rather than to benefit economically); (ii) it is waged with the right intention; (iii) it is waged by a legitimate authority;[3] (iv) it is the last resort; (v) it is proportionate (i.e., its morally good effects outweigh, or at least are not outweighed by, its morally bad effects); and (vi) it has a reasonable prospect of success (i.e., it is likely that the just end can actually be achieved by way of waging war).[4]

As a body of thought that aims to offer tools for both justification and critique, the tradition is often seen to be positioned between the political realist view that there is nothing to be justified morally about war – since subjecting war to moral judgement would be a category mistake – and the pacifist view that war is always and everywhere morally wrong. In the words of Tony

Lang and Cian O'Driscoll (cited in Rengger, 2013), 'the just war tradition manifests, on the one hand, a tragic resignation to the necessity of war in this fallen world, and, on the other hand, a determination to restrict its destructiveness'. But this is not the whole story. Rather, the tradition is 'at least as much about the promotion of justice, or at least the elimination of injustice, as it is about the limitations of destructiveness' (Rengger, 2013, 65).

In its purported attempt to promote justice and limit destructiveness, the just war tradition has been concerned not only with self-defence but also with the defence of others.[5] Indeed, this has been part of the just war tradition for a long time. In the early 16th century, Francesco de Vitoria (1991, 288, emphasis removed) argued that 'in lawful defence of the innocent from unjust death, even without the Pope's authority, the Spaniards may prohibit the barbarians from practising any nefarious custom or rite'; and that 'if they refuse to do so, war may be declared upon them'. According to David Fisher (2011, 223), who generously overlooks Vitoria's colonial mind-set, 'the doctrine [of just war] embodied a generous and altruistic vision of the purposes for which military force could be used: not just to protect one's own citizens but also to prevent the suffering of the innocent, wherever they were'.

While the idea of humanitarian war is far from novel, it has gained traction over the last few decades.[6] Even Walzer, who was initially quite reluctant to endorse humanitarian interventions, has come to embrace moral demands for them. In *Just and Unjust Wars* (1977), he (2006, 90–91) emphasised the importance of self-determination, demanding 'a kind of *a priori* respect for state *boundaries*'. 'Intervention is always justified as if it were an exception to a general rule, made necessary by the urgency or extremity of a particular case'. Humanitarian intervention can be justified *only*, he (2006, 106–107) then thought, 'when it is a response (with reasonable expectations of success) to acts "that shock the conscience of mankind"'. In a more recent publication, however, Walzer (2004, xii–xiii) considered his previous position too restrictive in light of conscience-shocking atrocities that occurred during the 1990s:

> Faced with sheer numbers of recent horrors – with massacre and ethnic cleansing in Bosnia and Kosovo; in Rwanda, the Sudan, Sierra Leone, the Congo, and Liberia; in East Timor (and earlier, in Cambodia and Bangladesh) – I have slowly become more willing to call for military intervention. I haven't dropped the presumption against intervention that I defended in my book, but I have found it easier and easier to override my presumption. And faced with reiterated experience of state failure, the re-emergence of a form of politics that European historians call "bastard feudalism", dominated by warring gangs and would-be charismatic leaders, I have become more willing to defend long-term military occupations, in the form of protectorates and trusteeships, and to think of nation-building as a necessary part of postwar politics.[7]

What seems to have triggered this development in Walzer's thinking is the Rwandan genocide in 1994, where 800,000 Tutsis and moderate Hutus were slaughtered during the course of 100 days. Walzer (2004, xi) is very clear that a military attempt to stop this genocide would have been a just war (2004, xi). Indeed, using language that resonates with the civilisational divide invoked by Vitoria, Walzer (2004, 81) insisted in the wake of Rwanda that 'it isn't enough to wait until the tyrants, the zealots, and the bigots have done their filthy work and then rush food and medicine to the ragged survivors. Whenever the filthy work can be stopped, it should be stopped'.

Walzer is joined in his embrace of humanitarian intervention by a growing number of cosmopolitan just war thinkers who do not share his *a priori* respect for state boundaries (see, e.g., Fabre, 2012; Lango, 2014). According to Cécile Fabre (2012, 170), 'a political regime has a claim to govern over a given territory only if it respects and protects the fundamental rights of its individual members'. While this insistence might still be compatible with

Walzer's presumption against intervention, cosmopolitan just war theorists 'deny ... that there is any intrinsic value to attach to communal sovereignty which would always dictate against intervention' (Fabre, 2012, 170).[8] This cosmopolitan turn in just war thinking reflects a broader trend that has established the individual, rather than the political community, as the ultimate unit of moral concern; the basic idea being that individuals ought to be protected regardless of where they are from. Individual rights are prior to any rights held by the groups that they form, and a political regime has moral status only if it protects these individual rights. As Fabre (2012, 8) puts it, cosmopolitan principles for a just war 'must ascribe pre-eminence to individuals and not conceive of groups as having independent moral status'. Indeed,

> a regime which violates the fundamental rights of its members undermines the very rationale for its existence and for its claim to authority, and thus forfeits its immunity from interference in its conduct; by implication, foreign communities are entitled to intervene militarily on behalf of its victims, subject to the latter's consent and considerations of proportionality. (Fabre, 2012, 170–171)

If a state is violating the rights of individuals on a large scale, it makes itself liable to military intervention in the sense that it has no right not to be warred upon. There is no difference here between the liability of an aggressor who attacks foreign innocents and the liability of an aggressor who attacks their own innocents at home.[9]

Introducing the Responsibility to Protect

Reflecting developments in just war thinking, international actors working to prevent and respond to mass atrocities have demonstrated growing commitment – at a rhetorical level at least – to the protection of individual rights. Since the inception of the UN there has been a tension between state sovereignty – the principle according to which states have ultimate control over their own territory – and the human rights of individuals. For these are rights that humans have regardless of which political community they belong to, and they therefore ought to be enforced by the international community if a state is unwilling or unable to enforce them. Whilst the principle (if not practice) of state sovereignty allowed states to do as they please in their own territory, human rights principles go in a different direction.[10] They suggest, at the very least, that mass atrocities are unacceptable crimes against humanity; crimes that, even if performed by or in a sovereign state, ought to generate some kind of international response. The increase in alleged practices of humanitarian military intervention in the 1990s heightened this long-standing tension.[11] A number of states – especially those that had won their sovereignty only recently after years of anti-colonial struggle – were worried that the emerging "right" of humanitarian intervention (or, as some called it, humanitarian imperialism) would undermine their hard-won state sovereignty (Bricmont, 2006; Chomsky, 2008).

This renewed tension between state sovereignty and the promotion of human rights through military intervention led Kofi Annan (2000, 49) – then Secretary-General of the UN – to ask: 'if humanitarian intervention is, indeed, an unacceptable assault on sovereignty, how should we respond to a Rwanda, to a Srebrenica, to gross and systematic violations of human rights that offend every precept of our common humanity?' To respond to this question, an International Committee on Intervention and State Sovereignty (ICISS) was formed. Their answer, detailed in a 2001 report, was the idea of a responsibility to protect. To reconcile so-called humanitarian military intervention with the principle of state sovereignty, the ICISS replaced an understanding of sovereignty as the right to unlimited control over territory with an understanding of sovereignty as responsibility. Though the ICISS was influenced more by Sudanese scholar and diplomat Francis Deng's (1995) idea of 'responsible sovereignty' than by cosmopolitan just war thinking, the effect of the principle is similar: sovereignty was rendered conditional on the protection of (some) individual rights. If sovereignty 'implies responsibility', sovereign status is conditional upon fulfilment of the state's responsibility to protect all individuals within its borders from mass atrocities. Whilst the 'primary responsibility for the protection of its people lies with the state itself', failure to protect effectively annuls this right to sovereignty as responsibility. In such situations – of manifest inability or refusal to protect populations from mass atrocities – 'the principle of non-intervention yields to the international responsibility to protect'. In other words, if a state is 'unwilling or unable' to protect people, responsibility shifts to the international community, which ought to take appropriate measures to protect the population including, as a last resort, military intervention (ICISS, 2001, xi).

The R2P was subsequently adopted, in a revised form, by the UN General Assembly in the World Summit Outcome Document of 2005 (UN, 2005). Its scope was limited to four mass atrocity crimes: genocide, ethnic cleansing, crimes against humanity and war crimes. The R2P has since framed international attempts to prevent and respond to mass atrocities.[12] As a broader framework for preventing and responding to mass atrocities, it addresses more than just humanitarian military intervention. It has three pillars (UN, 2009). The first pillar relates to the enduring responsibility of each state to protect their population from the four specified mass atrocity crimes. A state must do all it can to prevent such crimes and respond to early warnings of their emergence.[13] The second pillar outlines the responsibility of the international community to assist states in fulfilling their obligation to protect civilians. This assistance can range from norm dissemination and capacity building to the provision of peacekeeping forces (with permission from the state in which they operate). This does not necessarily mean that *all* forms of assistance fall under the R2P, however, with disagreement often surrounding the question of whether a particular form of assistance took place or should take place as part of the R2P.[14] Finally, the third pillar outlines a commitment, on behalf of the international community, to take timely and decisive action, in ways that are consistent with the UN Charter, when mass atrocities break out or when there are signs that they are going to break out. When a state is unable or unwilling to fulfil its responsibility to protect, or when it is the perpetrator of atrocities, the international community has a responsibility to take action, including military intervention as a last resort, to protect people at risk.[15]

In the eyes of its defenders, this new commitment, norm, framework and principle – it is seen to be all four and we will use each term as and where appropriate – has the potential to end mass atrocities 'once and for all' (Evans, 2009). Or, more modestly, it is 'slowly and imperfectly' 'starting to reshape international affairs' and hence offers 'the best chance in our own time' for improving international attempts to prevent and respond to mass atrocities (Bellamy, 2015a, 72; 1). By contrast, we claim that this framework is narrow and distorting, and that it fails to recognise the changes required to end mass atrocities. The problem with the R2P lies not so much in the broad ideas of sovereignty as responsibility, civilian protection, conflict prevention and international assistance but in the way in which the principle is framed. This framing is, first of all, narrow in that it focuses only on the four mass atrocity crimes. Second, it is distorting insofar as it presumes that the causes of mass atrocities are internal to the state in question. It therefore misses the role of the international community in generating conflict and, in so doing, hides from view the wider range of actions needed to prevent mass atrocities in the long term. This problematic framing of the R2P results in a limited understanding of what conflict prevention, civilian protection and international assistance might mean. It also leads to a defence of humanitarian military intervention that is politically naïve. On the one hand, the R2P occludes the role of the international community in generating conflict. On the other, its third pillar authorises military intervention by that same international community. As a result, the R2P legitimises military intervention that takes place in addition to, and is likely to reproduce, already existing and harmful practices of economic and political intervention.

This critique of the broader framework of the R2P does not entail a rejection of all of the ideas and practices that might be associated with it. The idea that sovereignty involves responsibility and that the international community has a duty to assist states in fulfilling their responsibility may, in principle, be perfectly sensible. In addition, some of the practices that are regarded – albeit contentiously – to form part of the R2P, including practices of conflict prevention, diplomacy and peace-making, may sometimes make a positive difference. But insofar as these practices fall within the overall framework of the R2P they are restricted and potentially even undermined by it. They would be better served outside of the R2P and in a different, anti-militaristic framework oriented towards the construction of a peaceful world.

1 | THE CATASTROPHIC FAILURE OF INTERVENTION IN LIBYA

On 17 March 2011, the United Nations (UN) Security Council adopted Resolution 1973, giving authorisation for the North Atlantic Treaty Organization (NATO) to use all necessary measures short of a foreign occupation to protect the people of Libya from potential bloodshed. It was the first time that the Security Council had authorised military intervention against the wishes of a recognised sovereign ruler for the explicit purpose of protecting people. For supporters, the Responsibility to Protect (R2P) was a decisive factor in enabling the intervention (Bellamy, 2015a). Moreover, intervention in Libya was 'a textbook case of the R2P norm working exactly as it was supposed to' (Evans, 2012). It was a 'spectacular step forward' (Evans, 2012), making it 'clear to all that the R2P has arrived' (ki-Moon, 2011). It should be met with a sense of 'success, vindication, satisfaction, optimism', for in Libya, R2P 'unquestionably worked' (Heinbecker, 2011; Evans, 2012). Similar claims were made long after NATO's intervention. Ramesh Thakur (2013, 69), a member of the International Commission on Intervention and State Sovereignty (ICISS) that gave birth to the R2P, claimed in 2013 that the outcome in Libya was 'a triumph for R2P'. Two years later still, Alex Bellamy (2015a, 94) argued that the intervention dealt 'an apparently decisive blow to the claim that R2P has changed nothing'.

In this chapter, we show that such analysis flies in the face of what actually happened in Libya. We begin by looking at the emergence of civil war, juxtaposing the reasons given for intervention with evidence of what was happening on the ground. We then look at the effects of the UN-authorised NATO intervention, showing how regime change quickly became the central aim of the intervention. Subsequently, we examine the overall effects of this purportedly triumphant intervention, looking at death tolls before and after the conflict, the effects of the intervention in prolonging it, the war crimes that were committed on all sides and regional spill-over effects. Finally, we outline the legacy of intervention: a legacy that has left Libya divided and rife with conflict.

The outbreak of civil war

NATO's intervention in Libya occurred in the context of the Arab Spring. After non-violent civil disobedience had unseated long-standing dictators in Tunisia and Egypt, protest spread to Libya. Citizens in the eastern city of Benghazi rose up against the 42-year rule of Colonel Qaddafi on 15 February 2011. The uprising spread, changing very quickly from protest to full-blown civil war. Rebels gained ground rapidly, taking a number of key Libyan cities and controlling, by 5 March, at least half of the country's populated areas. But Qaddafi's forces responded, pushing back the rebels and leaving them isolated in their initial stronghold in Benghazi. It was in this context that the UN Security Council agreed Resolution 1973, authorising the use of 'all necessary measures' short of foreign military occupation to protect civilians in Libya (UNSC, 2011).

Narratives of the Libyan intervention often take the following form. Peaceful protest spread to Libya only to be repressed by Colonel Qaddafi's security forces. The repression was violent and indiscriminate. Indeed, some stories – repeated by then International Criminal Court prosecutor Luis Moreno-Ocampo – suggested that Qaddafi had provided Viagra to soldiers in order to use rape as a weapon of war. Speaking to the UN, Navi Pillay, High Commissioner for Human Rights, said that reports indicated that 'thousands may have been killed or injured' (UN News, 2011). Worse yet, as Qaddafi was fighting back against the rebels, he (cited in BBC, 2011a) referred to the protestors as 'cockroaches'; a word previously used in extremist Hutu radio broadcasting to describe Tutsis ahead of and during the 1994 Rwandan genocide. Qaddafi promised to 'cleanse Libya house by house' to rid the country of rebellion. In the context of these emerging crimes against humanity, and with worries that there would be a bloodbath in Benghazi similar to those in Rwanda and at Srebrenica in 1995, the international community – with the support of regional organisations including the League of Arab States and the Organisation of Islamic Co-Operation – intervened.

This simple narrative of brutal killers, peaceful victims and humanitarian saviours was questioned at the time and does not stand the test of even the slightest scrutiny. First, the infamous Viagra rape claim turned out to be a fabrication developed by rebels in the hopes of inciting external military support (Cockburn, 2011; Kuperman, 2013).[1] Second, the rebels were not solely or exclusively innocent civilian victims. The Libya uprising, despite starting with peaceful protest *à la* rebellion in Tunisia and Egypt, swiftly turned into an armed uprising, with armed Islamists making up a substantial part of the rebellion. Third, whilst Qaddafi's words were chilling, they were spoken on 22 February, almost a month before Resolution 1973 and the NATO intervention. In the time between these comments and the NATO intervention, Qaddafi's forces had retaken a number of cities including Brega and Misrata (Kuperman, 2013). Reclaiming these cities was far from bloodless, but the death toll was significantly lower than Pillay had intimated. In Misrata, for instance, medical facilities documented a total of 257 people killed, including rebels and government forces (Human Rights Watch, 2011). Whilst it is true that weapons were also fired at unarmed protestors, this does not justify the comparisons that were made between Libya and the mass killings that took place in Srebrenica and Rwanda.[2] Finally, the simple narrative was based on a selective hearing of Qaddafi's words. When on the verge of launching an offensive to retake Benghazi, Qaddafi (cited in HCFAC, 2016, 14) also said:

> Throw away your weapons, exactly like your brothers in Ajdabiya and other places did. They laid down their arms and were safe. We never pursued them at all ... whoever hands over his weapons, stays at home without any weapons, whatever he did previously, he will be pardoned, protected.

In sum, there were not grounds to think that a Rwanda- or Srebrenica-like genocide was about to occur (HCFAC, 2016, 14–15). Such perceptions arose only through the 'very one-sided view of the logic of events' that had been presented; a view which mistakenly portrayed 'the protest movement as entirely peaceful', 'repeatedly' suggested 'that the regime's security forces were unaccountably massacring armed demonstrators who presented no security challenge', and picked up, without questioning, 'false claims or manufactured evidence' and large exaggerations of the numbers of casualties (International Crisis Group, 2011, 4; Cockburn, 2011).

NATO intervention

In the context of these sensationalised reports, the international community authorised all necessary measures to protect civilians. NATO was to take charge of the intervention. It quickly became clear that this was a mission aiming to reverse Qaddafi's gains and help the rebels – then on the verge of defeat – to an overall victory. NATO began an intensive bombing campaign against Qaddafi's forces and military infrastructure, bombing troops even as they were retreating and hence not providing an immediate threat to civilians. Very quickly, the dynamics of the war changed. Rebels – with further assistance from ground troops supplied in the 'hundreds in every region' by Qatar, expertise and intelligence provided by British officials, and weapons supplied by France – fought back and gained territory, only to be pushed back in turn by Qaddafi's forces (Qatar's military chief of staff, cited in Al Arabiya, 2011; HCFAC, 2016, 16–17; Kuperman, 2013).

NATO repeatedly rejected offers of a ceasefire from the Libyan government. Even before the intervention, Qaddafi had embraced Venezuela's offer of mediation but Jalil, the leader of the rebel forces, rejected the idea of holding talks (Al Jazeera, 2011). As the UN were discussing military intervention, the African Union was active in seeking to foster peace talks. It had arranged a meeting on 19 March, only for French President Sarkozy to arrange a summit for Libyan people on the same day in a clear snub to the African Union. African Union officials were told that their safety could not be guaranteed if they flew to Libya – by then a no-fly zone – to hold the meeting. Moreover, when the African Union did negotiate a ceasefire to which Qaddafi reluctantly agreed on 31 March, NATO offered no support to the plan, making it clear to the rebels that they could rely on NATO's backing even in the absence of any willingness to negotiate (De Waal, 2013). Emboldened by this seemingly unconditional support, the rebels continued to reject peace talks.

NATO's refusal to embrace peace talks led to accusations of "mission creep". Far from fulfilling a mandate to protect civilians – a mandate that would be best served through an immediate cessation of hostilities, peace talks, a negotiated settlement and a disarmament process – NATO appeared to be prioritising regime change. At a summit on 25 May, the African Union (2011, paragraph 51; see also De Waal, 2013) displayed anger at NATO's interpretation of the UN mandate for intervention, claiming that 'the pursuit of the military operations will not only undermine the very purpose' of Resolution 1973 – namely, the protection of civilians – but also 'compound any transition to democratic institutions'. Later, Brazilian UN representative Maria Viotti (2011) claimed that 'excessively broad interpretations of the protection of civilians ... could create the perception that it is being used as a smokescreen for regime change'. Similarly,

South African President Zuma (in Meo, 2011) said that Resolution 1973 was 'abused for regime change, political assassinations and foreign military occupation'.[3] NATO defended itself from such accusations, claiming that it was inconceivable that Libyan civilians could be protected with Qaddafi remaining leader (Coughlin, 2011).[4] Regime change was thus presented as a necessary means to pursue the end of protecting civilians. This claim, though, ignored the war crimes that were simultaneously being committed by the rebels, which indicated that civilians – especially those deemed loyal to Qaddafi – were unlikely to be protected under any government formed by the rebels. It also ignored fears, expressed by the African Union and then Chadian President Déby (cited in De Waal, 2013, 370), that a lack of negotiated transition would open 'the Libyan Pandora's box', in that it would lead to a vacuum of power that could see Libya's extensive arms stocks become accessible to rebels and militias. In turn, opening the Libyan Pandora's box would cause wider regional instability; fears that, as we shall see shortly, came true with the spill-over of conflict into neighbouring Mali.

A triumph?

With NATO supporting rebel forces and refusing peace talks, the Libyan conflict continued for a further seven months, "ending" on 23 October 2011, three days after the rape and execution of Qaddafi. Around 1,000 people had died from the fighting before the NATO intervention, at which point, as indicated above, it looked as though the war may have been at an end stage (Kuperman, 2013). By the end of the civil war, initial estimates by the new government of Libya – the National Transitional Council – suggested that around 30,000 had died. These were later revised to approximately 4,700 dead on the rebel side, a similar number dead on Qaddafi's side, and 2,100 missing (Black, 2013). The updated figures do not include civilian deaths. That estimates have varied so widely indicates just how difficult it is to get an accurate picture of the extent of killing that takes place in war.

But what is clear is that 'if the purpose of Western intervention in Libya's civil war was to protect civilians and save lives, it has been a catastrophic failure' (Milne, 2011).

Whilst the NATO bombing campaign itself was later deemed by the UN Office of the High Commissioner for Human Rights to be a 'highly precise campaign with a demonstrable determination to avoid civilian casualties', there were still notable civilian casualties (OHCHR, 2012, summary). Human Rights Watch (2012a) documented at least 72 civilian deaths from NATO air strikes. This figure includes the deaths of children, and includes an event at which 34 people were killed as NATO hit two family compounds that displayed no signs – aside from a single military coat found in the rubble – of any military activity. In this incident, NATO first hit the compounds with a bomb, with neighbours subsequently coming to help people who had been hurt in the explosion. NATO attacked again shortly afterwards while people were searching for the victims.

The NATO campaign also ensured a continuation of violence and human rights violations by Qaddafi's regime – fighting once more for its survival – and provided cover under which the rebels continued to commit 'war crimes and breaches of international human rights law', including 'unlawful killing, arbitrary arrest, torture, enforced disappearance, indiscriminate attacks and pillage' (OCHCR, 2012, summary). Black Libyans were wrongly perceived to be pro-Qadaffi mercenary fighters and were sometimes killed by rebels on the spot. This perception also encouraged the ethnic cleansing of Tawergha – a town populated largely by black Libyans. Six months after the end of the war in April 2012, Human Rights Watch reported that abuses around Tawergha and Misrata 'appear to be so widespread and systematic that they may amount to crimes against humanity' (Human Rights Watch, 2012b). Such stark racial violence had not occurred in Libya under Qaddafi's rule, repressive though it was.[5] To the day of us writing this chapter, Tawergha remains a ghost town.

As Chad's then President Déby feared, the intervention also had spill-over effects. A spill-over of weapons fuelled a new insurgency led by the National Movement for the Liberation of Azawad – a separatist movement of ethnic Tuaregs seeking to challenge years of perceived domination. The insurgency was spurred by fighters who had left Libya, some of whom were fully armed having been fighting with Qaddafi's forces or having gained access to Libya's weapons in the chaos of the civil war. This fighting, which intensified as Islamist rebels joined the hostilities, resulted in what Amnesty International (2012) described as 'Mali's worst human rights situation in 50 years' and led to a subsequent French intervention. The effects of opening the Libyan Pandora's box of weapons were not limited to Mali. A UN Security Council report of 2013 documented worries about weapons fuelling Islamist insurgencies across North Africa and the Middle East (UNSC, 2013). Up to 15,000 surface-to-air missiles were unaccounted for in February 2012. According to Western intelligence sources, some have gone to Niger where they have been obtained by Boko Haram, an Islamic State (ISIS) affiliated rebel group (Ignatius, 2012). Al-Qaeda's North African branch is stocking 'up on weapons that have moved out of Libya after' the overthrow of Qaddafi (Miller, 2012). And Libyan weapons have been bought by Somali buyers with a view to being used by Islamist rebels and pirates in north-east Africa (van der Meerwe, cited in Reuters, 2012). Overall, illicit transfers of Libyan arms have involved 'more than 12 countries and include heavy and light weapons such as portable air defence systems, explosives, mines, and small arms and ammunition' (Lederer, 2013).

Libya after the NATO intervention: is this what success looks like?

The Tripoli-based General National Congress governed Libya following an election in 2012. This government – like the NATO-supported rebels – contained large numbers of Islamists who voted to put into place Sharia law and to impose gender segregation in universities (Al Jazeera, 2013; Mahjar-Barducci, 2014). Some members were closely linked to the militias and armed groups involved in the uprising, and their rule was characterised by various disputes and security failings, including the high-profile assassination of a US ambassador in 2012 and the kidnapping of the Prime Minister in 2013 (Campbell, 2013). The General National Congress refused to stand down at the end of its electoral mandate in January 2014, voting to extend its own power. Discontent with this new Islamist-inspired rule soon led to renewed hostilities. In May 2014, renegade army General Khalifa Hafter launched Operation Dignity – a mission to eradicate Islamist and terrorist groups from Libya. Shortly after, new elections were held amidst increasing insecurity. Turnout was only 18 per cent. After suffering heavy defeats, Islamists rejected the results of the election. Islamists in the capital Tripoli and militias in Misrata then launched Operation Libya Dawn and seized Tripoli international airport. In this context, the disbanded General National Congress rejected the election result and reconvened (OHCHR, 2015; ECFR, 2016).

After these events, Libya was split between two rival parliaments, with a civil war between, on the one hand, General Haftar, the Libyan army and the House of Representatives based in Tobruk (who controlled much of the east) and, on the other, the General National Congress, supported initially by Libya Dawn militias, in the west. In addition, there have been numerous battles in the south of Libya between local armed militias – often with ever shifting loyalties between the eastern and western powers. Finally, so-called Islamic State took a major foothold in Sirte in the north of Libya (OHCHR, 2015, ECFR, 2016). This fighting and insecurity has resulted in: 'widespread violations of international human rights law and international humanitarian law, and abuses of human rights'; 'unlawful killings and executions; indiscriminate attacks, with an impact on civilians'; 'arbitrary detention'; 'torture'; 'sexual and gender based violence'; and 'violations of economic, social and cultural rights'. All of these were 'perpetrated by all parties to the conflict' (OHCHR, 2015, summary).

In an attempt to bring unity to the country, UN talks eventually resulted in the formation of a new Government of National Accord. This government initially had to be based in Tunisia as it had no support on the ground in Libya. It has since moved into Tripoli, with support from some of the militias that made up Libya Dawn and from some members of the General National Congress. Others in Tripoli, however, rejected the rule, which led to coup attempts in October 2016 and continues to stoke fears that the new government will face severe intimidation. Whilst the new unity government has pushed Islamic State back with support from the USA it is, at the time of writing this chapter, yet to be accepted by General Hafter or by the House of Representatives in Tobruk (ECFR, 2016).

Before the rebel uprisings and subsequent NATO intervention, Libya had the highest UN Human Development Index score of all African countries.[6] Now, according to the European Council of Foreign Relations (ECFR, 2016), 40 per cent of the population are in need of humanitarian aid and 60 per cent of the country's hospitals are inaccessible. As of February 2016, there were 435,000 internally displaced people – nearly one in 12 of Libya's six million people. There were 4,348 violent deaths between January 2014 and January 2016. The failures in Libya have not gone unnoticed, even by those that played a role in authorising the intervention. Obama (2016) called Libya a 'shit show' and a UK House of Commons Foreign Affairs Committee composed of MPs from the Conservative, Labour and Scottish National parties concluded that the intervention was 'not informed by accurate intelligence'. The UK government, the report continued, 'failed to identify that the threat to civilians was overstated and that the rebels included a significant Islamist element'. Moreover, the 'intervention to protect civilians ... drifted into an opportunist policy of regime change' which, in turn, 'was not underpinned by a strategy to support and shape post-Qaddafi Libya'. Ultimately, the intervention resulted in 'political and economic collapse, inter-militia and inter-tribal warfare, humanitarian and migrant crises, widespread human rights violations, the spread of Qaddafi-regime weapons across the region and the growth of ISIS [Islamic State] in North Africa' (HCFAC, 2016, summary).

The killing of civilians, rampant war crimes, the ethnic cleansing of Tawergha, mass displacement, a country in dire humanitarian need and conflicts over power: is this what success looks like? Is this an example of the R2P working exactly as it was supposed to? Is this a clear sign that the R2P has made an important and progressive difference in world politics? Far from being a great success, the Libya intervention appears to have increased killing, generated mass displacement and fostered instability in Libya and beyond.

Despite all of this, some continue to defend the Libya intervention on the basis that, in light of Qaddafi's talk of cleansing Libya of cockroaches, failure to intervene would have led to a bloodbath akin to Rwanda or Srebrenica. Relatedly, Hehir (2016) and Vilmer (2016) suggest that without military intervention, Libya could have turned into another Syria. In other words, the intervention was justified on humanitarian grounds because things would have been even worse had it not taken place. This claim is based only on conjecture and speculation. Given that it is mobilised to justify the pursuit of actions with devastating effects, it requires – at the very least – a robust evidential base and a compelling set of reasons as to why things would have been worse in the absence of intervention.

There is always uncertainty with this kind of counter-factual analysis – an analysis of what would have happened if an event that occurred had not taken place (or an analysis of what would have happened if an event that did not occur had taken place). Nonetheless, some counter-factual analyses are more robust than others, and there are good reasons to believe that we will not be provided with robust evidence and compelling reasons as to why Libya would have become another Srebrenica, Rwanda or Syria. Indeed, we saw that comparisons with Rwanda and Srebrenica were based on a selective reading of Qaddafi's words and failed to analyse his actions in reclaiming other towns and cities; actions that, whilst violent, indicated that he was far more likely to act on his promise to pardon those that drop their weapons than engage in Srebrenica- or Rwanda-like mass killing. Moreover, Qaddafi had reclaimed a number of cities without the degree of bloodshed later witnessed as Assad reclaimed Syrian cities. And he was on the verge of taking back the last remaining rebel stronghold in Benghazi. Given the speed with which Qaddafi's forces had retaken other cities, one would expect that Benghazi would have been reclaimed very quickly, if not as quickly as the 48 hours predicted by Colonel Qaddafi's son, Saif al Islam (cited in Black, 2011). Alan Kuperman has offered a counter-factual account of what would have happened without intervention by extrapolating from what actually happened, and not from what was feared in light of one-sided, worst-case scenario media reports and snippets extracted from Qaddafi's speeches. He found that the NATO intervention magnified the conflict's duration about sixfold and its death toll at least sevenfold, even before taking into account the instability that has come back to plague Libya in the years following the "end" of the war.[7] The Libya case indicates that interventions – even those deemed a triumph for R2P – have devastating effects.

2 | AS THE WORLD BURNS, WE BATHE IN THE GLORY OF A NEW NORM OF PROTECTION

The Libya intervention was a catastrophic failure. But defenders of the Responsibility to Protect (R2P) deem it a triumph. How is this misjudgement possible? In this chapter, we suggest that it stems from an approach that separates the evaluation of the R2P from what is happening in the material world. The R2P is a principle that operates in real existing world politics and is intended to regulate real interventions that have enormous impact. Despite this, analyses of whether actual interventions do more good than harm are conspicuous by their relative absence, and support for the R2P more broadly is based on abstract arguments that fail to engage with the realities of war. What is taken to be a measure of success is not whether attempts to prevent and respond to mass atrocity crimes are working but the extent to which an international "norm" has emerged. In the first section, we indicate that the R2P is not a new legal principle but an international norm or standard of appropriate and expected behaviour. This norm is deemed able, by its supporters, to change the values, practices and identities of states in world politics. We then show how focus on the development of the R2P as a norm comes at the expense of any analysis of its material effects, before arguing that this approach resulted in the catastrophic misjudgement on Libya. In the second section, we suggest that this abstract approach is replicated in defences of the wider record of the R2P. Amidst increases in the very violations that the R2P is meant to address, its supporters claim that it is facilitating progress in how the international community is responding to mass atrocities. While the choir has been singing the praises of the R2P, direct physical killing in conflict has increased.

Norm-based idealism

After emerging in the report of the International Commission on Intervention and State Sovereignty (ICISS) in 2001, the R2P was debated at the 2005 United Nations (UN) World Summit meeting. This meeting was billed as the largest gathering of world leaders in history. It saw heads and representatives of 191 states come together to make a series of decisions about the future of the UN. The World Summit produced an outcome document reaffirming a series of fundamental principles and advancing some new ones. Included in the document were two heavily debated paragraphs on the R2P which affirm the following: first, every state has 'a responsibility to protect its populations from genocide, war crimes, ethnic cleansing and crimes against humanity' (pillar one). Second, the international community has a duty to assist states in meeting this responsibility and in preventing mass atrocities (pillar two). Third, the international community, through the UN, has a responsibility to 'take collective action, in a timely and decisive manner', in order to protect people in other states when those states are 'manifestly failing to protect their populations from genocide, war crimes, ethnic cleansing and crimes against humanity'.[1] Such timely and decisive collective action must take place 'through the Security Council, in accordance with the [UN] Charter ... [and] on a case-by-case basis' (UN, 2005, 138 and 139).

When accepting its responsibility to protect, the international community did not commit to any new legal obligations. The UN Charter – including its commitment to state sovereignty and its claim that it is legitimate to intervene in states only for reasons of self-defence and international security – was not changed. Similarly, the veto power of the five permanent members of the Security Council – China, France, Russia, the UK and the USA – remained unchecked. The R2P therefore 'did not change ... the basic international rules governing the use of force; it 'has not ... in any way altered either the structure of the international legal system, its laws, or the decision-making process' (Bellamy, 2015a, 14; Murray and Hehir, 2012, 392). Moreover, the commitment made was to take action only on a case-by-case basis. This went against one of the objectives of the 2001 ICISS report, which was to overcome the perceived inconsistency that saw military intervention take place in some cases (i.e., Kosovo) but not in others that were similarly grave or indeed graver (i.e., Rwanda). As such, the ICISS had set out general criteria for intervention, aiming to ensure that when these were met the international community had an *obligation* to act on behalf of victims, rather than a right to intervene that could be used selectively. In light of the commitment to act only on a case-by-case basis, this 'revolutionary import' of the R2P 'all but vanished'. It was replaced with a 'precedent-denying' phrase that neither compels action in mass atrocity situations nor – given that any action is taken explicitly on a single-case basis – allows room for consistent action to set legal and moral precedent for future action (Hopgood, 2014, 204).[2]

It perhaps comes as little surprise, then, that the R2P failed the first tests of whether it would generate meaningful action and change responses to mass atrocities. The crisis in the Darfur region of Sudan – where militants armed and supported by the Sudanese government were engaged in acts of ethnic cleansing against Fur peoples – continued apace as the R2P was adopted. The new acceptance of the R2P did not change the gridlock that had prevented significant action. Similarly, in 2009 during the final months of a long civil war between Tamil independence fighters and the Sri Lankan government, hundreds of thousands of Tamil civilians were trapped in territory held by the Tamil Tigers, having been forced to leave with the fighters as they were retreating. The Sri Lankan government, claiming it was involved in counter-insurgency against a terrorist group, engaged in mass shelling of Tamil areas. The UN remained largely silent as up to 70,000 civilians were killed (UN, 2012a). A report investigating the failures in Sri Lanka suggested that whilst the concept of a responsibility to protect 'was raised occasionally during the final stages of the conflict', it was raised 'to no useful result. Different perceptions among member states and the Secretariat of the concept's meaning and use had become so contentious as to nullify its potential value'. As such, 'making references to the Responsibility to Protect was seen as more likely to weaken rather than strengthen UN action' (UN, 2012a, paragraph 74).

For supporters of the R2P, however, everything was about to change. In 2009, the Secretary-General wrote the first of a series of annual reports further specifying the meaning of the R2P. This report was discussed and approved by the General Assembly. Later in the same year, the Security Council agreed resolutions 1970 and 1973 on Libya, the second of which authorised, for the first time, the use of force for the purpose of protection against the wishes of a recognised sovereign state (see Bellamy, 2015a, 93–95). These resolutions and the entirety of the international response were, for Bellamy (2015a, 95), 'suffused with R2P'; members of the Security Council and UN officials 'repeatedly' used the 'language of the R2P' during negotiations. 'The 2011 intervention in Libya' thus 'dealt an apparently decisive blow to the claim that R2P has changed nothing' (Bellamy, 2015a, 94). It showed that the R2P had arrived and had started to make a difference.

As we know from Chapter 1, the Libya intervention increased killing and human rights violations, generated regional instability and dismantled Libya. How is it possible to consider such an intervention to have '*unquestionably* worked', as co-commissioner of the ICISS Gareth Evans (2012, emphasis added) put it? The answer, we suggest, lies in the abstraction endemic in discussions of the R2P. For its defenders, the R2P is a new norm – a standard of appropriate behaviour that states in "international society" are expected to adopt and act in accordance with. The idea is that whilst a state might initially commit only rhetorically to a norm – like a norm according to which crimes that shock the conscience of humanity are unacceptable – this very rhetorical claim will, over time, create limits on possible justifications for action. These limits may well go on to mould states' action and, in time, shape their identity. Starting to profess a new norm of protection – of one's own population and of others – may thus be the "thin end of a wedge" that leads states to change their identity such that they protect their populations from atrocity crimes and refuse to "stand aside" as atrocity crimes take place in a distant land.

From this perspective, what ultimately matters is the language used by states in high-level discussions. If states adopt new norms – even if only at a discursive level to begin with – these norms can grow in significance and start to have effects on behaviour. The focus of analysis in celebrations of the R2P, then, is on high-level discourse. The Libya intervention was judged to be an unquestionable success not because of what happened on the ground in (and in the air above) Libya but because of what happened in the UN Security Council. There, for the first time (and according to R2P advocates because of a growing commitment to the R2P), a military intervention was authorised against the wishes of a recognised sovereign authority. The R2P is considered to have worked in the sense that it encouraged the international community to take action for the purpose of protection. The "success" of what actually happened on the ground and in the air is simply presumed.

To understand the methodological abstraction which underlies support for the R2P, a primer on norms is required. The R2P is not a new legal principle. Instead, it is what constructivist international relations theorists call a norm, or a standard of appropriate behaviour. We live in a society that is governed both by formal legal rules that can be enforced through courts and more informal social norms that can be enforced through praise, stigma, isolation, social approval or disapproval and so on. There is, for instance, no law suggesting that a person cannot watch a football match while attending a funeral and cheer loudly as their team scores. Such behaviour, though, is not considered acceptable. Were someone to engage in it they would probably be rebuked and asked to stop. They might be shamed afterwards. And if they were to engage in such behaviour again, they might even be excluded from the relevant social circle (let alone from future funerals). Most social norms regulate behaviours so ordinary that we simply do not notice them. Through years of socialisation, we have come to act in ways that are appropriate without thinking about it. Social norms, and the forms of approval and disapproval that come with appropriate or inappropriate behaviour, change our behaviour and eventually come to shape our identity as a person.

For English School and Constructivist International Relations theorists, norms matter in international and global politics. There is such a thing as an international society or a society of states. This society is governed by a set of international norms: standards 'of appropriate behaviour for actors with a given identity' (Finnemore and Sikkink, 1998, 891). States and state representatives engage in various normalised forms of behaviour, whether that be appropriate ways of speaking (and not speaking out of turn) in high-level meetings or certain modes of interacting with one another. In addition to these expected, everyday forms of behaviour, states also regard certain *ideas* and *moral values* as appropriate. Ideas and norms therefore matter in world politics. If an idea – be it an idea of state sovereignty, an idea of the value of civilian protection, or an idea that hunting whales in danger of extinction is wrong – is adopted by international society as a normalised, expected standard of behaviour, then that idea will have an effect by regulating the behaviour of states and other actors. For its supporters, the R2P has power as an international norm, or at least potential to have such power. It may not have legal clout, but it can become an expected standard of behaviour which will lead to approval (when it is met) and disapproval (when it is not). It may eventually change the identity of states such that they would *not even consider* acting in a manner that contravenes their responsibility to protect. Belief that the R2P will generate major change in world politics, then, 'is predicated on an assumption that normative pressure ... will compel the Permanent 5' members of the Security Council and other states in international society 'to alter the foreign policy calculus' (Averre and Davies, 2015, 817).

Constructivist theorists have developed an account of how international norms emerge and develop. International norms have a 'life-cycle' (Finnemore and Sikkink, 1998; Shawki, 2011). The first stage is the emergence of the norm. Here, the principle develops and comes to the attention of international society, sometimes through the work of "norm entrepreneurs" – people or groups that develop a new norm and apply pressure on international society to adopt it. In the case of the R2P, the norm was developed in the ICISS report, drawing on existing norms of humanitarian intervention advocated by former Secretary-General Kofi Annan amongst others. It quickly came to the attention of the UN, being discussed in the General Assembly in 2004 before being included in the World Summit Outcome document in 2005. Since then, the Secretary-General, the Special Advisor on the R2P and a range of academic and policy advocates have continued to act as norm entrepreneurs through annual statements by the Secretary-General, continued advocacy work and the production of vast amounts of literature. The second stage is that of a "norm cascade". At this stage, acceptance, at the rhetorical level at least, spreads rapidly among countries that have yet to accept the norm. As we shall see shortly, the R2P has generated this rhetorical assent very quickly.

Agreement in principle and/or at the level of rhetoric does not immediately change behaviour. A number of states may have adopted the principle out of a sense of pressure; a sense that they would be stigmatised were they not to accept the norm. Whilst such acceptance may not be meaningful at first, it can, for R2P supporters, come to have significant effects. First, once they have adopted the principle, Security Council members 'cannot make any argument they want' on the basis that the R2P places 'limitations on appropriate discourse' (Walling, 2015, 388). This is so because 'members will incur reputational costs if they advance arguments that do not reasonably justify their conduct in relationship to legal or moral norms' (Walling, 2015, 388). Or, put differently, 'the motivations states may have for supporting R2P may be driven by interests that have nothing or little to do with responsible sovereignty', but 'where this is the case such states leave themselves open to scrutiny and censure' (Dunne and Gelber, 2015, 227). Rhetorical affirmation thus opens the door to further social pressure, which may eventually force a change in action. Second, anyone who wants to force a state into action – whether it be another state, a humanitarian NGO, a UN official or a social movement – may be able to use a state's rhetorical affirmation of the principle against them, demanding that they practise what they preach. If such pressure is effective, the rhetorical affirmation of a norm would, albeit indirectly, work to change the actions undertaken by states. Changes in discourse, then, eventually generate changes in behaviour. Changes in both discourse and behaviour will, in turn, have an impact on the identity of states (and other actors) in international society. Much as the repeated performance of social norms gives them a normalised quality such that we perform them without thinking, the repeated performance of international norms will eventually mean that they are taken for granted. And much as we see social norms – insofar as we are aware of them at all – as an important part of our identity, international norms eventually become a key and unquestioned part of a state's identity. On this account, if the R2P grows as a norm, states will eventually see themselves as actors that do not engage in atrocity crimes and act decisively when others do.[3]

The key to the success of a norm, then, is rhetorical assent, changed behaviour and changed identity. Whether or not success in these three respects has been achieved is judged through a focus on discourse in high-level international meetings, notably in the UN Security Council and General Assembly. A decision to take action for humanitarian purposes is taken – without reference to the realities of that action on the ground – as a mark of changing behaviour. We learn from reading literature on the R2P, for instance, that the principle was adopted in the World Summit Outcome document of 2005. We learn that there have been annual debates on Secretary-General reports since 2009 and that over the years more and more states have expressed agreement with the broad outlines of the principle. The debate now concerns not whether there is agreement on the principle but how it should be implemented (UN, 2012b). We learn that 'little or no opposition to the principle remains among member states' (Luck, 2011a, 389). Indeed, only a few hard-line dissenters – namely Algeria, Belarus, Bolivia, Cuba, Ecuador, Iran, Nicaragua, North Korea, Pakistan, Sudan, Syria, Venezuela and Zimbabwe – remain (Quinton-Brown, 2013). We learn that China and Russia – states that are often regarded as being highly sceptical of any principle that could undermine traditional understandings of state sovereignty – have cast more votes in favour of the principle at the UN than the majority of Western democracies (Bellamy, 2015a, 2). We learn that between 2005 and 2015, the Security Council adopted 30 resolutions and six presidential statements referring to the R2P (UN, 2015a); that over a period of 15 months in 2010/2011, the Special Advisors on the prevention of genocide and on the R2P issued eight public statements on situations of particular concern (Luck, 2011b); and that 'the Secretary-General has invoked the R2P with even greater frequency' (Luck, 2011b, 392). Finally, we see failures re-branded as signs of growing acceptance of the norm. As Bellamy (2015a, 100) puts it, 'pronounced criticism of failures', such as the failure of protection in Sri Lanka, 'suggests that R2P is starting to set the standard against which future actions will be judged'.[4]

We also get a sense of what we, as scholars and activists, should do. For Quinton-Brown (2013, 262), it is important to address the reasons as to why dissenter states continue to object to the R2P because 'by obstructing international consensus, all R2P dissenters inhibit the normative development of R2P by rhetorical means'. 'The goal of addressing dissent', he continues, is to 'build consensus on R2P and facilitate its development as an international norm' (Quinton-Brown, 2013, 277). 'If the international community is unable to control dissent, then the principle will struggle to push through its norm cascade and fail to satisfy the technical definition of an international norm, much to the detriment of its own perceived legitimacy' (Quinton-Brown, 2013, 261). We hear calls for 'a far better understanding of local context ... enabling more culturally appropriate and effective applications of the R2P norm in the future'. These more culturally appropriate applications will, in turn, help ensure 'an even more robust R2P normative cascade' (Mani and Weiss, 2011, 455). We even learn that we should not move too quickly to insist that the permanent five members of the Security Council refrain from using their veto in the event of mass atrocities. Bellamy (2015b, 177) claims that it is 'perhaps no bad thing in the short term' that there are not stronger calls for the permanent five members of the Security Council to exercise veto restraint; restraint that the ICISS had deemed key to ensuring that interventions in mass atrocity situations were not blocked, as they frequently are through Russian vetoes on Syria and US vetoes on Palestine. This is no bad thing because 'pressure on the veto could weaken consensus on R2P by reawakening concerns about the norm's capacity to extend the legitimation of force beyond the prevailing status quo' (Bellamy, 2015b, 177). These statements all presume that what is important is that the norm can grow further.

Why is there so much at stake in the question of whether the R2P norm is being accepted and adopted? By generating this normative, idea-based change, the R2P is capable, for Evans (2009), of 'ending mass atrocities once and for all'. The R2P is effectively socialising states into a fundamental belief that mass atrocities are not acceptable, ought to be prevented, and demand a timely and decisive response when they do break out. This socialisation will, in turn, lead to behaviours that respect and do justice to this principle of protection. Finally, such behaviours will eventually become a taken-for-granted part of states' identity; a reflex action akin to – say – dressing up for a wedding or holding the door open for someone directly behind you. Bellamy is more circumspect. A norm like the R2P can 'reshape (but not determine) behaviour'. Norms operate alongside other factors, including interests that are less benign. Someone may be in such a hurry to get to the front of a queue that they do not hold the door open for someone else, even though they have been socialised into doing so and deem letting it close on someone inappropriate and unacceptable. As a result, 'there is no silver bullet to the problem of genocide and mass atrocities and R2P does not purport to provide one'. What it does offer, though, is 'a set of shared expectations about appropriate behaviour that may, over time, make the world less tolerant of mass atrocities and more protective of its victims' (Bellamy, 2015a, 17–18). Bellamy's view is shared by Ban ki-Moon who, in his 2015 report (UN, 2015a, paragraph 62), said that 'the growing acceptance of the responsibility to protect now makes it much more difficult for the Security Council to justify inaction in the face of genocide, war crimes, ethnic cleansing and crimes against humanity'. Ultimately, for Bellamy (2015a, 1), this normative acceptance means that the R2P 'offers the best chance in our own time to build an international community that is less tolerant of mass atrocities and more predisposed to preventing them'. This 'optimism is based on the fact that R2P has achieved something that other projects aimed at eliminating genocide and mass atrocities have not: genuine and resilient international consensus'.

At this stage, readers may be shocked that optimism about and justifications of the principle focus entirely on elite-level discussions. Even more shocking is the manner in which this methodological abstraction continues in accounts of the 'triumph' of Libya (Thakur, 2013, 69; Evans, 2012). What is at stake in debates over Libya is not whether the North Atlantic Treaty Organization (NATO) intervention was effective in protecting civilians, but whether the R2P norm played an important role in the decision to intervene. In a typical example, Marie-Eve Loiselle (2013, 317, emphasis added) 'examines the situation in Libya, and in particular whether the *language of Security Council Resolutions* 1970 and 1973 suggests that the measures adopted were contingent upon the belief in the existence of a responsibility to act to prevent crimes against humanity'. 'The situation in Libya', here, refers to debates in the Security Council and the resultant language of resolutions concerning Libya. Loiselle's article contains only a very brief overview of the crisis in Libya and, as is typical of R2P scholarship, takes this overview only as far as Qaddafi's threat of atrocities on the eve of the NATO intervention (see, for instance, Bellamy and Williams, 2011; Dunne and Gelber, 2014 and 2015; Mohamed, 2012; Shawki, 2011; Thakur, 2013). The Libya intervention is hailed as a great success not because of what actually happened on the ground. Rather, it is hailed as a success because 'R2P played a significant role in the public debate that occurred up to the passage of resolutions 1970 and 1973'; because it was 'a decisive factor in galvanizing the consensus inside the chamber of the Security Council' (Dunne and Gelber, 2015, 226; see also Bellamy, 2015a, 95; Sahnoun, 2011; Thakur, 2013; Williams, 2011).

It is this abstract approach that results in the catastrophic misjudgement according to which the Libya intervention was 'a textbook case of the R2P norm working exactly as it was supposed to' (Evans, 2012); 'an unprecedented moment', making it 'clear to all that the R2P has arrived' (Williams, 2011, 249; ki-Moon, 2011); a 'spectacular step forward' (Evans, 2011); 'a triumph for R2P' (Thakur, 2013, 69); the dawn of a 'more humane world' (Axworthy, 2011); something that reveals a 'new politics of protection' (Bellamy and Williams, 2011). It is this abstraction that encourages scholars to embrace the Libya intervention with a sense of 'success, vindication, satisfaction, optimism' (Heinbecker, 2011); to regard it as a 'triumph for R2P', showing that 'it is possible for the international community ... to deploy international force to neutralise the military might of a thug and intervene between him and his victim' (Thakur, 2013, 69). All of this because, in light of the authorisation of intervention in Libya, 'R2P is coming closer to being solidified as an actionable norm' (Thakur, 2013, 72).

At the abstract level at which R2P scholarship and policy advocacy operate these claims may well be true. It might be the case that the R2P did change discussions in a manner that ultimately changed behaviour and led to UN-authorised action where it would not have been taken before.[5] But this says nothing at all about what actually happened in Libya. Libya was regarded as a triumph because the new idea and principle of R2P changed debates, perceptions and ultimately behaviours within the Security Council to the point that, for the first time, it authorised intervention for the purpose of protection against the wishes of a recognised sovereign authority. The *idea* of the R2P mattered in generating intervention. The *material reality* of the intervention drops out of the picture.[6] As a result, scholars have 'largely overlooked the more practical question of whether and how international military action can avert mass atrocities' (Paris, 2014, 569).[7]

Despite this lack of engagement with the practical question of whether military intervention can avert atrocities, Bellamy (2015a, 40) claims that 'big steps by concerned outsiders can save lots of lives. I can say this with a degree of confidence thanks to the work of others. The positive effects of outside intervention have been proven by several studies'. Bellamy's confidence is based, however, on a highly selective reading of relevant studies. He cites four studies, of which only two actually argue that humanitarian military intervention can save lives.[8] Of these two studies, one does not share Bellamy's confidence, claiming instead that 'it is necessary to be ruthlessly modest about what humanitarian intervention can do' (Seybolt, 2007, 276). To state that the positive effects of outside intervention have been proven occludes the contested nature of data on intervention and ignores studies that yield very different findings. Peksen (2012, 558), for instance, found that 'military intervention contributes to the rise of state repression', measured in terms of the levels of 'extrajudicial killing, disappearance, political imprisonment and torture'.[9] We are not, here, suggesting that one particular study is right and another is wrong. We are simply indicating that, as Hafner-Burton (2014, 276) puts it in a review of social scientific literature on human rights, 'there is no broad consensus' concerning whether military 'interventions are effective or defensible policy to protect human rights'.

The failure to analyse the facts on the ground that is endemic in scholarship on the R2P is replicated in policy circles. A study conducted in 2006 on military planning in NATO, the UN and a number of Western governments found 'little well-developed or well-known doctrine addressing operations authorised to use force to protect civilians under imminent threat' (Holt and Berkman, 2006, 103; see also Paris, 2014, 571). Even the UN Special Advisor on the R2P claims that whilst the 'jury is still out' on the question of whether the R2P has made a material difference, his '*unscientific feeling* is that the R2P has saved lives by helping to discourage further violence against populations in Kenya, Kyrgyzstan, Guinea, Cote D'Ivoire and Libya' (Luck, 2011a, 393, emphasis added). One would hope that actions of such gravity as sustained bombing campaigns would be based on more than an unscientific feeling that they might make a difference; that advocacy for a principle that, as a last resort, allows for military intervention would be based on rigorous analysis of the effects of such intervention. Moreover, given that a key factor in deciding whether to intervene is said to be whether there is a reasonable prospect of a good humanitarian outcome, this kind of analysis is a *responsibility*, especially amongst those defending and acting as Special Advisor on the principle. Calls for the development of the R2P, and calls for other-defending war more broadly, require an analysis of the material realities of war. It is only in the absence of such an analysis that it is possible to claim, in blind and irresponsible ignorance, that Libya was a success and that outsider intervention is known to save lives. And as we shall show in the next section, it is also only on the basis of such ignorance that it is possible to claim that the R2P is improving international responses to mass atrocities.

The wider record of the Responsibility to Protect

Alex Bellamy (2015a, 72–74) claims that criticisms of the R2P suffer from focusing 'only on a small subset of cases – mainly Darfur, Libya, and Syria'. To understand the wider record of the R2P it is important to 'consider the totality of the Security Council's work'. When this totality of work is explored, Bellamy argues, it becomes clear that 'R2P is starting to reshape international affairs'. Albeit 'slowly and imperfectly', it is 'facilitating more fundamental changes to the values, identities and thus to the interests of states and societies themselves'. A growing number of states recognise that committing atrocities is incompatible with their responsibility, as sovereigns, to protect civilians. The failure to condemn or act in response to mass atrocities is, moreover, becoming the exception rather than the norm. There are therefore 'clear signs of underlying progress', even as some outlier cases do not exhibit any of these signs. In this section, we point out that these signs of progress are present only at the abstract level of the development of the R2P norm. When it comes to the material world, evidence points in the other direction. The R2P is not associated with any improvement in attempts to prevent and respond to mass atrocity crimes.

Bellamy's claim that there are signs of underlying progress is based on data on responses to mass atrocities over time. He focuses on whether the international community is more or less willing to become engaged when atrocities occur. Using data from the Uppsala Conflict Data Program, Bellamy identifies all situations involving high rates of one-sided violence against civilians in armed conflict between 2006 and the end of 2014. He then examines whether the R2P was mentioned in Security Council discussions concerning the crisis and whether there was a Security Council Resolution in response. This is done to identify *not* whether international responses to atrocities were adequate or helped the situation but to see whether the R2P works as a 'rallying call', inspiring the Security Council to agree to a resolution. Left out of the picture is whether any given resolution authorised effective steps to respond to the crisis.[10] Bellamy (2015a, 68) found that 'the Security Council adopted resolutions in a little under two-thirds (63%) of the cases of mass atrocity where R2P language was used'. This is almost double the 'strike rate' of 33 per cent in cases where R2P language was not used. 'So', Bellamy concludes, 'the Security Council is nearly twice as likely to adopt measures when a situation involving mass atrocities is framed in R2P terms than when it is not'.

In light of the discussion of norm-based idealism in the previous section, one problem with Bellamy's method immediately becomes apparent. What Bellamy measures is not the kind or effectiveness of action taken on the basis of the R2P. Rather, he measures the association between talk about the R2P and the existence of a Security Council resolution. This simply means that where there is more talk – more discussion about the case and hence more likelihood of the R2P being mentioned – there is more talk, this time in the form of a UN Security Council resolution. In other words, the data does not suffice to show that significant action was taken, let alone that the action responded effectively to mass atrocities. By taking this approach, Bellamy reaches findings that are counter-intuitive, to say the least: Syria and Yemen, commonly regarded as abject failures, end up being read as cases in which R2P "worked", simply on the basis that R2P was mentioned and resolutions were adopted.[11]

What if, instead of looking at data on whether R2P works as a rallying call, we bring reality back in and look directly at the extent of killing in one-sided conflict? What we would see, using the Uppsala Conflict Data Program database that Bellamy draws on – limited as it may be – is that there was a large increase in direct killing in one-sided violence after 2011; the very year that Bellamy identifies as key in embedding the R2P.[12] More broadly, when it comes to looking at the extent of armed conflict in the world, 'for the past ten years … the Uppsala Conflict Data Program has recorded an uneven, yet clearly visible, upward trend', with a particularly notable upward trend in the 'number of internationalized armed conflicts' (Pettersson and Wallensteen, 2015, 536). This has resulted in a growing number of fatalities through direct killing in conflict. 'The trend' of a decline in violence, which Bellamy (2016) has cited as evidence of the R2P working, 'seems to have now been reversed' (Pettersson and Wallensteen, 2015, 536). The R2P is correlated, then, with a notable increase in fatalities in one-sided violence and in battle-related fatalities of all types, particularly in internationalised armed conflict. Our point here is not to say that the R2P has *caused* these worsening levels of violence (though the instability and spill-over that stemmed from the Libya intervention in 2011 may go some way to account for them). It is simply to say that the R2P has not been associated with improvements in attempts to prevent and respond to mass atrocity crimes. As the new UN Secretary-General António Guterres said in his first annual report on the R2P (UN, 2017), 'the number of civilians subjected to atrocity crimes, including women and children, has increased significantly over the past few years', as have 'violations of [relevant] human rights and international humanitarian law'. When we step away from abstract reflection on Security Council discourse and go back to the reality of civilian protection, we see that the wider record of the R2P is a record of failure.

◆ ◆ ◆

While Libya has gone from being the most prosperous state in the region to a failed state subject to protracted conflict, and while killing in atrocity crimes has increased significantly, supporters of the R2P have been bathing in the glory of a new norm of protection. They have claimed that the Libya intervention was an unquestionable success and that the wider record of the R2P is one of a slow and imperfect improvement in international responses to mass atrocity. This catastrophic misjudgement – of both the Libya intervention and the wider record of the R2P – is based on an approach that focuses only on high-level discourse and not on the realities of humanitarian military intervention and civilian protection. Once we bring the material reality of war and civilian protection back into the picture, we see that other-defending wars like the war in Libya are not just, humanitarian and protective, and that the R2P is failing in its stated purpose of preventing and responding to mass atrocities.

Deleting reality: abstraction in contemporary just war thinking

While defenders of the R2P engage in forms of abstraction that celebrate the emergence of a norm irrespective of the material realities of war, just war theorists distort their object of analysis by engaging in abstract thought experiments.

A number of contemporary just war theorists use experiments that involve individuals in contexts that do not have anything to do with war (see Fabre, 2012; Frowe, 2011; Kamm, 2012; and McMahan, 2009).[13] One such experiment, as we will discuss further in Chapters 3 and 5, involves children drowning in ponds under the eyes of potential saviours. Cécile Fabre (2012, 13) shows awareness of the methodological problems of using such thought experiments, admitting that 'there is something to be said' for claims according to which 'hypotheticals ... are too abstract and too detached from reality to be of much use; indeed, by grossly distorting what really is happening in the real world, they can have the pernicious effect of justifying practices which ought never to be condoned'. Alas, she proceeds anyway. And the reason she offers is merely that 'if used sparingly and judiciously, hypotheticals do help us to isolate morally relevant features of particular cases and thereby uncover our intuitions'. But this is precisely the problem: the idea that we can isolate morally relevant features of particular cases. For particular cases are inseparable from their social and political context.

In isolating what are taken to be relevant moral variables and appealing to our apparently shared (yet covered) intuitions about them, theorists think that such conjectures can help us make reliable moral judgements about war. What is driving this epidemic use of such thought experiments is the idea that these experiments can somehow reduce or eliminate our political bias:

> Like many philosophers, I often use fictional examples to illustrate ideas pertaining to war. This might strike some readers as odd – surely, we might think, history is full of real-life examples that could better serve this purpose. But

(continued)

(continued)

> using fictional examples helps us identify principles that
> can be obscured by the complexities of historical cases. For
> example, many people have firm views about the morality of
> the United States. Using a historical example that concerns
> the actions of the United States might thus throw up more
> questions than it solves if we are tempted to evaluate those
> actions on the basis of what we already know or believe
> about a particular case. When we're trying to identify general
> rules or principles, we want to abstract from features that
> might exert an illicit influence on our judgements. Fictional
> cases help us to do this. (Frowe, 2011, 2)

The complex material world is seen here as a disturbing factor that introduces 'bias' and encourages 'unhelpful disputes
over historical details' (Lazar, 2017). It can therefore only get
in the way of making firm judgements about the morality of
war. Just war theorists engage in forms of abstraction that
see the gaining of theoretical clarity as the relevant measure
of progress regardless of the state of the material world in
which such progress takes place – much as defenders of the
R2P see the emergence of and consensus around an abstract
international norm as the relevant indicator of progress. What
drops out of the picture is the material world, which tends to
ruin the party.

Thought experiments are ideologically charged in that
they take for granted a methodological individualism: the idea
that we can theorise about the responsibilities and liabilities
of individual persons and individual states in neatly separa-
ble historical situations; that we, the moral commentators,
can give any US war a fair chance of being morally justified:
a chance that is not tainted by our views – and indeed our
knowledge – of the kind of global actor the USA is and the
kinds of interventions it has previously been involved in.[14] In

that sense, thought experiments are always eminently political. They have a particular disposition written into them, one that favours a moral evaluation of idealised, rational and atomised agents over a consideration of the way in which these agents are historically and structurally connected.[15] Individuals and communities are not just seen to be operating on an equal playing field – which, given the magnitude of global inequalities, is far from being the case. They are also seen as disconnected until the very moment at which the thought experiment begins. This methodology, as Fabre recognises in principle but not in its drastic implications, profoundly distorts the material world. And any suggestion that thought experiments can be designed such that these distortions are eliminated – for instance by accommodating for power relations and trying to approximate the material world more and more (until we get a roughly accurate picture) – leads to a very good question: why not start with the material world, real politics and real people(s)?

It is for this reason that we started, in Chapter 1, with a real war. What we see in real wars is arbitrary killing, rape, mass displacement, extensive human rights violations and the spread of instability. This is all a far cry from the sanitised thought experiments common in contemporary just war thinking, and indeed from the celebration of norm development in R2P scholarship. The horrors of Libya render more difficult an account according to which wars can be just, much as they serve to render bizarre, not to mention downright offensive to its victims, a description of Libya as a triumph.

3 | ZONES OF CIVILITY AND ZONES OF BARBARISM: THE INTERNALIST DIAGNOSIS OF MASS ATROCITY CRIMES

Recall George Osborne's (in Wintour, 2016a) words on the crisis in Eastern Aleppo. The crisis emerged in 'a vacuum of Western leadership' and demonstrated 'the price of not intervening'. According to this narrative, atrocity crimes simply crop up as a result of barbarism or failings in other parts of the world. Onlookers then face that infamous choice: intervene or stand aside. Osborne is not alone in understanding atrocity crimes in this manner. His way of thinking is also written into just war thinking and the Responsibility to Protect (R2P). This chapter exposes the narrow and distorting way in which just war thinking and the R2P frame atrocity, its prevention and appropriate responses to it. Both see the emergence of mass atrocities as a result solely of dynamics that take place "over there"; dynamics that are internal to the part of the world in which atrocity is taking place.[1] This internalist diagnosis results in an understanding of mass atrocities – and of their prevention – that is blind to the ways in which purported saviours are already intervening. Consequently, it obscures and marginalises the deep responses – ending unfair trade, reducing inequality, ending land grabbing and so on – that are necessary for the prevention of mass atrocity crimes.[2]

This brief chapter proceeds as follows. We begin by outlining the way in which leading just war theorist Michael Walzer divides the world into zones of barbarism and zones of civility. This division, we argue, is replicated in the principle of and policy concerning the R2P, serving to restrict options for addressing atrocity. Finally, we identify how this framing of atrocity leads to calls for actors to intervene militarily regardless of their potential contributions to the emergence of the very crisis that they are called upon to resolve.

♦ ♦ ♦

Walzer (2004, 81) identifies two 'source[s] of the inhumanity' that might lead the 'supposedly decent people on this planet' to intervene. One is 'external and singular', such as 'a tyrant, a conqueror or usurper, or an alien power set over against a mass of victims'; the other is 'internal', by which Walzer means 'locally and widely rooted, a matter of political culture, social structures, historical memories, ethnic fear, resentment, or hatred'. In this analysis, absent invasion by a tyrant/usurper, mass atrocities result from the barbarism or failings of a society. Walzer tells a simplistic moral story in which he assumes two essentially disconnected zones: a zone of the 'supposedly decent people' and a zone of barbarism and/or failure. 'No doubt the "civilized" world is capable', Walzer (2004, 74) claims, 'of living with grossly uncivilized behaviour in places like East Timor, say – offstage and out of sight. But behaviour of this kind, unchallenged, tends to spread, to be imitated or reiterated. Pay the moral price of silence and callousness', he continues, 'and you will soon have to pay the price of turmoil and lawlessness nearer home'. What Walzer (2004, 74–75, emphasis removed) is particularly worried about is a process in which 'terrorist regimes in the third world imitate one another (often with help from the first world), and waves of desperate refugees flee into countries where powerful political sources, not yet ascendant, want to drive them back. For how long will decency survive here, if there is no decency there?' In as much as international causes of atrocity are recognised, they are only a parenthesis, a point of lesser significance, in a story that otherwise separates the barbaric Third World from the decent First World.

There are continuities between Walzer's just war thinking and the R2P. Key policy-influencers working on the R2P also suggest that mass atrocity situations emerge owing to problems internal to the place in which they occur. Ramesh Thakur (2013, 62), a member of the International Commission on Intervention and State Sovereignty (ICISS), replicates this framing of the problem, stating that 'the principle of the R2P is an acknowledgement by all who live in zones of safety of a duty of care towards those in zones of danger'. Thakur describes the R2P as a mechanism which provides 'vulnerable groups' with 'protection from predations by brutish rulers domestically'. More specifically, he (2013, 69; see also Luck, 2011a, 394) asserts that the Libyan intervention was launched in order 'to neutralize the military might of a thug and intervene between him and his victims' – a diagnosis that, as Chapter 1 demonstrated, was based on sensationalised and in some cases false media reporting.

This internalist diagnosis continues, albeit in a more nuanced way, in a series of annual UN Secretary-General reports detailing the state of play of the R2P and synthesising policy measures that have been taken in order to enhance protection.[3] In a report focused on international assistance, there is virtually nothing drawing attention to already existing international interactions that, as we shall argue in the following chapter, lead to conflict. Instead, the focus falls on building domestic capacity, providing encouragement and offering assistance. Capacity might be built through the creation of: 'a processional and accountable security sector; impartial institutions for overseeing political transitions; independent judicial and human rights institutions; the capacity to assess risk and mobilise early response; local capacity; media capacity; and capacity for effective and legitimate transitional justice' (UN, 2015a, n20; UN, 2014). Similarly, encouragement might involve: peer review of activities and prevention mechanisms in a vulnerable state; 'awareness raising and norm dissemination'; 'the dissemination of human rights and humanitarian standards and norms'; the 'education of national authorities'; and 'confidential or public dialogue to remind states under stress of the importance of meeting their responsibility to protect' (UN, 2014,

29–31).[4] All of these measures relate to problems that exist "over there", in the state in question. There is no sense that other states might need to change their own practices; no sense that potential supporters need to alter the ways in which they – or people and companies within them – already interact with states "over there" in a manner that puts the latter under the very stress that can lead to atrocity. The entire report presents only one exception when it mentions that the international community has a role to play in restricting the flow of arms, illicit financing and illegal trafficking (UN 2014, 58). This sense that states have a responsibility to change forms of action that contribute to atrocity crimes is to be welcomed. As will become clear in the following chapter, however, it only scratches the surface of the range of ways in which already existing interventions generate conflict and suffering.

When constructed as separate from an expected or occurring atrocity, the international community is left with a choice. It can either be a 'bystander to genocide', manifestly failing to act upon stated commitments to human rights and civilian protection (Power, 2001). Or it can intervene, whether through building preventative capacity, disseminating humanitarian norms, offering humanitarian assistance, brokering negotiations or engaging in full-scale military intervention. R2P scholarship and public discourse are rife with these choices. In Rwanda, Srebrenica and Syria, the international community is lambasted for standing aside, generating the 'vacuum in … leadership' that George Osborne (in Wintour, 2016a) so misleadingly refers to in his speech on the crisis in Aleppo. In Kosovo and Libya, the international community is celebrated for its willingness to act. Other states thus enter the picture either as passive bystanders or as active saviours. As Anne Orford (1999) has pointed out, this framing of the problem of mass atrocities is gendered. It tells a masculinised story in which heroic saviours, coded as male, use military means to save passive victims, coded as female.[5] It is also, as Mamdani (2010) and Pourmokhtari (2013) argue, a racialised and neo-colonial framing which splits the international system between, on the one hand, safe and predominantly white states that have responsibilities beyond their territory and, on the other hand, dangerous and predominantly post-colonial states that are in need of external protective intervention.[6]

This framing of atrocity also lies behind calls for actors to intervene militarily regardless of their prior and ongoing involvement. When Walzer (2004, 74–75) states that 'terrorist regimes in the third world imitate one another (often with help from the first world)', he literally brackets the not-so-decent complicity of the supposedly decent in the actions of the indecent others. This bracketing reflects a consequential choice on Walzer's part; it is not some sort of "objective" representation of the material world. He is entirely aware, for example, of 'the involvement of the West in the production and reproduction of inequality'. Indeed, he considers the role it plays 'fairly large' (Walzer, 2004, 132). He does not, however, establish any link between involvement of the West and the inhumanities that he thinks call for humanitarian military intervention. By conveniently bracketing the indecency of the 'supposedly decent', Walzer (2004, 81) gives the impression that such indecency cannot be sufficiently relevant a consideration to threaten the integrity of his moral and political case for intervention.[7]

A younger generation of just war theorists do not fare much better on this front. Cécile Fabre is not oblivious to some of the operating mechanisms of the material world. She (2012, 101) is aware, for instance, of 'the tendency of ... highly developed countries to prop up corrupt regimes for the sake of continued access to prized resources'. She (2012, 102) also alludes to 'protectionist measures designed by the affluent to protect their own markets from Third World countries' exports'; 'patenting restrictions on vital medical treatments, particularly AIDS'; 'cripplingly heavy debt repayments for bad loans pushed on [Third World countries] by the affluent for geostrategic reasons'; and affluent countries 'supporting dictators who plunder their own country's natural wealth and divert aid payment to nefarious military pro-grammes, or worse, their personal bank accounts'. And yet, she mentions these things only in the context of defending the claim that subsistence wars can, in principle, be just: that 'the very deprived have a just cause for going to war against the affluent if the latter are in breach of their ... duties of justice to them' (2012, 112). Her recognition of the interconnectedness of issues of mass atrocity and structural injustice – and of the involvement of purported humanitarian saviours in the production of these injustices – does not survive beyond her reflections on subsist-ence wars.

With the injustices of patents, protectionism, unfair debts and support for dictators deleted from the picture, Fabre goes on to discuss the ethics of humanitarian military intervention. Humanitarian wars need *not* be fought 'purely for altruistic reasons', nor do the parties who wage them need to be 'rights-respecting communities' (Fabre, 2012, 167; 189). Using an analogy of a child drowning in a pond, Fabre points out that a murderer is not forbidden from saving the child on account that they are a murderer. 'What matters, rather, is that he should be able to swim and recuse the child effectively – and then hand her over to appropriate parties' (Fabre, 2012, 189). Relatedly, she believes that self-interest and failure to be a rights-respecting community in other respects can be reconciled with moral con-duct for the purpose of effective military protection – a point we shall return to in Chapter 5. She (2012, 185) is aware that 'humanitarian interventions ... are never waged solely out of concern for the victims; rather interveners have their own, self-interested reasons for financing the war and exposing their troops to its risks'. But she does not consider this political fact to have significant bearing on her moral analysis. Yes, self-interest taints humanitarian wars, but it does not make them impermissible (Fabre, 2012, 185–186). The imperative to stop the immediate massacre trumps considerations about who intervenes and with what agenda: 'when multinational institutions are ... derelict and cannot or will not mobilise forces and funds quickly enough to avert rights violations on a mass scale (as was the case during the Rwandan genocide), the right to wage war may be held by whomever is in a position to protect the victims' (2012, 188).[8] Who wages the wars is at most a side consideration, for Fabre, in part because of her prior move of placing other injustices in a separate analytic box. With these neatly parcelled out, any recognition that the interveners themselves might be implicated in the violations drops out of the picture.

In the rare moments in which Fabre does recognise this prior and continuing involvement, she reconfigures it as a factor which potentially strengthens the case for humanitarian wars to be waged by those that contributed to the problem in the first place. She (2012, 190) points to the fact that 'France, a long-term supporter of the extremist Hutu regime of President Habyarimana, supplied the Rwandan regular army with weapons as well as technical and strategic expertise not merely in the months leading up to the genocide, but as the massacres had already started'. Her (2012, 190, n32) accusation is that 'the French were negligently unwitting abettors of the genocide'. But the reader is immediately informed that this does not in any way disqualify the French from intervening militarily. On the contrary, 'in such cases it might stand to reason that France had a primary responsibility to intervene in the genocide as early as April 1994 – just as it behoves me, out of all available rescuers, to help the child I negligently pushed into the water' (2012, 190).[9] What Fabre fails to realise is that, as we shall explore further in the remaining chapters, arms exports are a deep-rooted and widespread phenomenon, not marginal, isolated and happening out of negligence.[10] For her, France's unwitting contribution to the Rwandan genocide is some sort of anomaly; an aberration that gives rise to a special responsibility – effectively to kill to protect – such that France can compensate for its "negligence".

If she were instead to recognise arms trading as a deeply embedded and widely practised feature of the foreign policy of great powers, she might begin to ask, as we do in Chapter 5, whether it is sensible to give abettors of genocide additional responsibilities to protect people through military means.

For the most part, however, the affluent are not conceived of as harm-doers but as potential helpers. As Fabre writes, 'if the affluent are under a duty to fund the delivery of food, medical supplies, engineering expertise, and so on, for the sake of helping distant strangers, then it would seem that they are under a duty to protect the latter from harm by way of humanitarian intervention' (Fabre, 2012, 181). Protectionism, patents, plunder: they fall off the radar in Fabre's (2012, 161) analysis of the 'deep morality' of humanitarian intervention. The assumption is, quite simply, that 'the beneficiaries of humanitarian intervention are victims of *someone else's* wrongdoing' (Fabre 2012, 182, emphasis added).

As we shall make clear in the next chapter, this is emphatically not the case. By leaving behind the narrow and distorting framework of analysis that we find in just war thinking and the R2P, we are able to explore ways in which agents that often present themselves as humanitarian saviours are already intervening in a manner that stokes conflict. This exposure reveals two important things. First, in light of the way in which these actors generate conflict and atrocity they are not – contra Fabre – fit for the purpose of humanitarian military intervention. Second, there are multiple ways in which states can change how they intervene in a manner that can help prevent the emergence of mass atrocity crimes.

4 | EVERYDAY ATROCITY AND ALREADY EXISTING INTERVENTION

Resort to the use of force as a response to security and humanitarian crises continues to mean that insufficient attention is paid to the extent to which the policies of international institutions themselves contribute to creating the conditions that lead to such crises. (Orford, 1997, 681)

Focus on crisis both displaces and distorts attention to "the everyday", whether it be "everyday" killing, rape, hunger, or gross wealth disparity. It also reinforces a pre-realist understanding of intervention: imagining a world in which not acting militarily is "not acting", and refusing to see the ways in which many of the same powers that ultimately send in the troops have often played a significant role in creating conditions ripe for a crisis. (Engle, 2007, 224)

The Responsibility to Protect (R2P) and contemporary just war thinking both focus only on mass atrocities involving direct physical violence. They also imagine a world in which the international community is not involved in such atrocities until the moment at which they face a choice between "acting" and "standing aside". What happens if we widen the gaze and bring into the picture the everyday atrocity of mass avoidable death? After all, death on the scale of the Rwandan genocide takes place through hunger alone as a feature of the routine functioning of the contemporary global order. As shall become clear in this chapter, this death is not a mere accident, nor is it unavoidable. It is produced politically. 'Built into the structure[s]' of world politics is a violence that 'shows up as unequal power and consequently as unequal life chances' (Galtung, 1969, 171).[1] What if we bring into the picture violent global political structures and the already existing practices of intervention that (re)produce them? In addition to widening the gaze in this manner, this chapter suggests that everyday atrocity generates conditions in which war crimes, ethnic cleansing, crimes against humanity and genocide are more likely to occur. Far from being separate issues that should be left to other academic debates and other policy frameworks, global injustices and the interventions that reproduce them must be placed at the centre of any analysis of human protection.

This chapter is divided into six sections. The first highlights the extent of everyday atrocity. The remaining five address, respectively: the production of "under-development"; environmental destruction; land grabbing; the stoking of ethnic tensions; and arms trading.[2] In each section we suggest that already existing interventions cause the atrocity of mass avoidable death and – sometimes demonstrably, sometimes apparently or at least potentially – create conditions in which mass atrocity crimes thrive. We illustrate these points by reference to a number of cases in which the four mass atrocity crimes with which R2P is concerned were committed. Our purpose here is not to offer a comprehensive analysis of any of these cases. Rather, we use them illustratively to show how the aforementioned factors – land grabbing, arms trading and so on – contribute to atrocity.

Three further caveats are in order. First, in claiming that everyday atrocity and already existing interventions help create a world conducive to mass atrocity crimes, we are not saying that such crimes have a single cause or that given factors – "under-development", environmental destruction, land grabbing, ethnic tensions – lead to them inevitably. Violent conflict is complex and has multiple causes. Indeed, even discussing these causes in their complex combinations does not fully address the question of why people are driven to violence in some cases and not in others (see Barnett, 2000). Emphasising the importance of underlying factors, then, does not exonerate or excuse the perpetrators of genocide and ethnic cleansing. It is simply to say that their abhorrent actions often occur in a political context that can and should be changed. Second, providing an exhaustive analysis of these issues within a single book, let alone a single chapter, would be impossible. We present only a broad overview, and readers are encouraged to follow extensive references to explore in more detail the empirical and historical evidence on which our claims are based. Third, our emphasis on mass avoidable human death is not meant to sideline the fact that already existing interventions and structural forms of violence have extremely serious non-lethal effects on people's lives. Nor is it meant to ignore that they have serious effects on the environment and on non-human animals. These impacts are of immense importance. But they tend to be occluded in just war thinking and the R2P, which focus only on direct and primarily lethal violence committed against humans. What is offered here is an anthropocentric understanding of violence that operates in a distorting framework governed by numbers of people killed in conflict alone. What we offer in the remainder of this chapter begins to depart from this framework. It should not be considered a definitive treatment, not least because everyday atrocity is not just about human death.

Everyday atrocity

In 2015, more than 16,000 children aged under five died every day. That's nearly six million during the year. According to the World Health Organization, 'almost all of these children's lives could be saved if they had access to simple and affordable interventions' (WHO, 2017a). This problem is not confined to the global South. In 2014, over 562,000 deaths in the European Union could have potentially been avoided with health care systems offering timely and effective medical treatments. A larger number of deaths – close to one million – could have been prevented through better public health interventions (Eurostat, 2017).

These numbers dwarf the estimated 152,000 people killed directly in wars and conflicts in 2015 (WHO, 2017b, 32).[3]

Whilst some global health indicators have shown notable improvements – child mortality has fallen by more than 50 per cent since 1990 (WHO, 2015) – the same cannot be said for hunger and poverty. Extreme poverty, defined by the World Bank (albeit contentiously) as living on less than $1.90 per day, affects 767 million people or 10.7 per cent of the world's population (World Bank, 2016). Whilst this number has decreased, it has done so primarily because of poverty reduction in China on the one hand and methodological fiat on the other. Real and globally inclusive progress has not taken place. Moreover, this poverty line sets an extremely low bar. The World Bank itself recognises that it is suitable only as a measure of poverty in the poorest countries. To give some indication: in Mexico in 2010, government figures based on a national poverty line reported that 46 per cent of the population were in poverty, whilst the World Bank, using its international poverty line, had the figure at 5 per cent (Hickel, 2017, 48). When the poverty line is moved up only slightly, we find that over three billion people – nearly half of the world's population – live in poverty (DS, 2017). If we shift further to what scholars have identified as an "ethical poverty line" – a line indicating the estimated amount of money required to achieve the lower end of normal life expectancy – we find that 4.3 billion people live in poverty (Edward, 2006; Hickel, 2017, 50). That is more than 60 per cent of the world's population. On these more appropriate measures, the number of people in poverty has 'been growing steadily over the past decades' (Hickel, 2017, 2; see also Hickel, 2016). All this during a period in which the wealth of the richest has grown dramatically: 42 billionaires now have as much wealth as 3.6 billion people – half of the world's population (Oxfam, 2018). Regional divides have grown too: 'the gap between the real per capita incomes of the global North and the global South has roughly tripled in size since 1960' (Hickel, 2017, 2).

US Secretary of State Henry Kissinger promised in 1964 that hunger – then effecting an estimated 460 million people worldwide – would be eradicated within a decade. In 2016, 815 million went hungry – an increase from 777 million in 2015 (FAO et al., 2017). As with poverty, baselines are very low. A person is considered hungry only if their calorific intake is 'inadequate to cover even minimum needs for a sedentary lifestyle' over the period of one year (FAO et al., 2012, 50). As the UN Food and Agriculture Organization – the organisation responsible for measuring hunger – points out, 'many poor and hungry people are likely to have livelihoods involved in arduous manual labour' (FAO et al., 2012, 12). The actual number of hungry people is thus likely to be much higher than the self-proclaimed 'narrow' and 'conservative' Food and Agriculture Organization estimates (FAO et al., 2012, 50; 55). If we measure hunger at a level that allows for "normal" activity levels, around 1.5 billion people go hungry. If we measure it for the intense activity levels associated with manual labour, the number stands at 2.5 billion (Hickel, 2017, 48). All this before we even begin to consider adequate nutrition.[4]

Estimates suggest that in the Rwandan genocide – a genocide that shocked the world with its sheer scale and rapidity – 800,000 people died in 100 days of killing. Conservative estimates suggest that a person dies for hunger-related reasons every 10 seconds.[5] This means that more than 800,000 people die from hunger *every* 100 days. This alone, without taking into account other deaths stemming from environmental conditions and avoidable disease, amounts to a mass atrocity that takes place as a matter of routine each and every day.

The international production of "under-development"

Since ethnic and regional tensions have been rising due to the conditions created by debts, economic crisis and adjustment, no strategy of conflict resolution will prove adequate and sustainable unless it tackles those underlying conditions. (Adekanye, 1995, 372)

In light of mass atrocity taking place every day, and in light of such everyday atrocity vastly outstripping the mass atrocities considered under the R2P in terms of the number of people affected, why is it that those supporting just wars and the R2P focus only on war crimes, ethnic cleansing, genocide and crimes against humanity? One possible explanation is that these avoidable deaths from hunger, poverty and treatable illness are regarded either as accidents or as something that stems from local features of corruption and poor institutions. Robert Kaplan (2001), for instance, presents a picture of a barbaric world of conflict driven by both ethnicity and rapacious demand for control over resources. Such conflict forebears a 'coming anarchy' to be addressed, Kaplan suggests, through new forms of colonial trusteeship. This view, however, does not hold up to scrutiny. Far from being locally produced, everyday mass atrocities are intimately related to intervention in a world profoundly shaped by colonial and post-colonial forms of violence. In 1500, prior to the colonisation of the Americas, the stark international inequalities that shape life chances in terms of geographical location of birth did not exist. They have come to exist by virtue of "development" pursued in one part of the world through forms of exploitation, extraction and domination that simultaneously rendered other parts of the world "poor" and "under-developed" (Escobar, 1995; Frank, 1966; Leech, 2012; Rodney, 2012).[6] The story of the emerging divide starts with the discovery, conquest and destruction of Latin America:

> With the conquest of the societies and cultures which inhabit what today is called Latin America, began the constitution of a new world order, culminating, five hundred years later, in a global power covering the whole planet. (Quijano, 2007, 168; see also Dussel, 1995)

By 1650, the continent's population had gone from around 90 million to 10 million as people were killed in battle, as

Europeans brought new diseases, and as populations were over-worked to the point of exhaustion and vulnerability to disease (Dussel, 1995; Galeano, 2009). Far from being an accidental by-product of Europe's rise, this death and destruction brought with it the gold, silver, free labour and additional land that was crucial to economic growth (Anievas and Nişancıoğlu, 2016; Dunford, 2017; Dussel, 1995; Frank, 1966; Hickel, 2017; Lugones, 2010; Mignolo, 2011). Later, the slave trade and colonialism in Asia and Africa further stretched global divides (Davis, 2002). As colonialists knew full well, violence else-where was integral to the economic and political development of colonial and imperial powers: 'if you want to avoid civil war, you must become imperialists', said Cecil Rhodes (cited in Brantlinger, 1988, 34). Land in the colonies provided a way of settling supposedly surplus populations; colonised people provided a market for goods; and the extraction of resources enabled wealth to grow, placating demands for unequally shared goods at "home". Even as formal colonialism ended, the USA and others, fuelled by Cold War rhetoric that pre-sented the policies of some newly independent Third World countries as a step towards communism, started to intervene. In Iran, Guatemala, Brazil, Chile, Indonesia, Ghana, the Democratic Republic of Congo and beyond, the US staged or supported coups deposing popular leaders and in many cases replacing them with military dictators and/or corrupt client regimes (Galeano, 2009; Heller, 2006; Jonas, 1991). It is through this long history of intervention that major global inequalities, and the poverty and "under-development" so prevalent on the underside of them, were *made* (Escobar, 1995; Frank, 1966).

"That's all well and good", you may say, but "doesn't the international community now provide aid and save strangers"? It is here that we meet another possible reason as to why every-day atrocity does not fall under the gaze of just war thinking and the R2P; namely, the view that oppressive North–South relations are a thing of the past that is now being addressed through aid, development and even peacebuilding. Roland Paris, for instance, claims that contemporary peacebuilding, though still a "civilising mission" in the sense that it exports liberal values across the world, differs from the "civilising mission" of colonialism. Whilst colonial powers were net extractors of wealth and resources, peacebuilding sees resources flow from North to South (Paris, 2002; 2010).

It is true that a significant amount of money is spent on aid, development, peacebuilding and so on. For instance, $128 billion of aid is sent to less developed countries every year. This transfer, however, is 'a mere trickle' when compared with 'the financial resources that flow in the opposite direction' (Hickel, 2017, 25). The Centre for Applied Research et al. (2015) have calculated all of the financial resources transferred between rich and poor countries each year. In 2012, the last year of recorded data, $2 trillion moved from developed countries to developing countries through foreign investment, aid, trade, debt cancellation, remittances and capital flight. $5 trillion went in the other direction. Developing countries thus 'sent $3 trillion more to the rest of the world than they received' (Hickel, 2017, 25–26). If we add up all of the transfers since 1980, these net outflows total $26.5 trillion. These outflows include payments on debts and capital flight. This capital flight is a product of lax financial regulation and the continued existence of tax havens, including the vast network of tax havens organised around the city of London (Brooks, 2014). The mechanisms may not always involve the stark direct physical violence of colonial rule, but a world of radically unequal life chances continues to be 'actively created' (Hickel, 2013). It is created in part through the actions and omissions of actors – transnational corporations, foreign governments, international organisations, trade associations and others – on a global stage.

Violence, showing up in these unequal life chances, remains embedded in the structures of contemporary world politics.

Everyday atrocity is not an accident, nor is it locally produced. But is it relevant to mass atrocity crimes? Might it not be the case that these issues are better addressed separately, in different academic debates and in different policy frameworks? Some scholars and practitioners may specialise in how to prevent and respond to directly physically violent mass atrocities, while others work out how to effectively tackle (or how to stop continually reproducing) poverty.[7] This approach – discussed in the previous chapter – runs into problems very quickly, for links between "under-development" and conflict are well established. During his stint as Secretary-General of the UN, Kofi Annan (UN, 2004, viii) pointed out that

> development and security are inextricably linked. A more secure world is only possible if poor countries are given a real chance to develop. Extreme poverty and infectious disease threaten many people directly but they also provide a fertile breeding ground for other threats, including civil conflict.

Annan's statement was based on research, performed for the World Bank by Paul Collier and others, which suggested that 'the risk of civil war is much higher in low-income countries than in middle-income countries' (Collier et al., 2003; see also Fearon and Laitlin, 2003; Krause and Suzuki, 2005). The reproduction of a structurally violent world in which the atrocity of mass avoidable death takes place as a matter of routine thus also creates conditions in which the four mass atrocity crimes continue to occur. It is a mistake to keep these two things separate. Any answer to the question of how to prevent and respond to atrocity crimes must also be an answer to the question of how to prevent and respond to prevailing conditions of structural violence: conditions that provide the ideal habitat for directly physically violent events to emerge. Indeed, already existing interventions were important background conditions in two cases central to arguments in defence of military intervention: Rwanda and the former Yugoslavia (Orford, 1997).

The Rwandan genocide arose in the context of a cocktail of conditions conducive to violent conflict including – as discussed later in this chapter – land pressures and ethnic divides that were magnified through colonial rule. Economic factors, stemming from a combination of domestic and international dynamics, also played an important role. Rwanda was one of a number of African states affected by the Third World debt crisis in the 1980s. The government took out loans from the World Bank which were conditional on adopting a Structural Adjustment Programme (SAP). SAPs have been widely criticised for 'kicking away the ladder' of development and re-entrenching poverty in affected countries (Chang, 2002). They have been shown to worsen government respect for physical integrity rights (Abouharb and Cingranelli, 2006).[8] And they have created conditions in which the very crimes that the R2P is concerned with thrive.

In Rwanda, there had been a long-standing perception, encouraged and promoted by Hutu elites, that Tutsis dominated in the market and Hutus in the state. SAPs call for a reduction of the state and better terms for private sector investors. In calling for less state and more market, SAP reforms were thus perceived to be shifting a delicate balance away from Hutus and towards Tutsis. This perception emerged in the context of an economic crisis that was amplified by, without being solely attributable to, structural adjustment. In the months after the adoption of the SAP, the Rwandan Franc suffered 40 per cent devaluation. Inflation rose sharply, with prices for a range of basic necessities in capital city Kigali rising by an estimated average of 50 per cent during the first seven months of structural adjustment (Waller, 1993, 33). At the same time, adjustment measures reduced government spending, which led to the elimination of transfers that had been given to coffee producers to ensure that they received a stable income in the midst of changing coffee prices. All of this at a time when the price of coffee – a product on which Rwandans depended heavily – was crashing on global markets, in part because of the breakdown of an International Coffee Agreement that had placed quotas and price controls on major coffee importers and exporters in order to stabilise prices (see Kamola, 2007). The loss of state support thus amplified already emerging livelihood pressures for a large number of Rwandans. Such pressures – along with rising ethnic tensions, land pressures and Hutu-elite inspired hatred of Tutsis – helped create the environment in which genocide broke out (Kamola, 2007). The Rwandan genocide, so often cited as a paradigmatic case of the tragedy of non-intervention, took place in the context of extensive intervention.

Take also the case of the former Yugoslavia, which took out an International Monetary Fund loan in 1984 in order to address an emerging economic crisis. SAP reforms put into place a stringent austerity programme which deepened the economic crisis and removed protections against large-scale unemploy-ment. They thus resulted in "ordinary people" feeling a growing sense of insecurity through rapid inflation, falling real incomes, shortages of basic goods and high unemployment. SAP reforms also enforced institutional changes which shifted the balance of economic policy in favour of particular republics and moved economic and political authority from republican governments and banks to the Federal Government and the National Bank. The reforms, which continued 'even with clear signs of civil war emerging', thus 'fuelled' the emerging 'nationalist dynamic'. They did so by eroding the sense of national unity that had been backed up by the government's provision of economic and administrative support, and by destroying mechanisms for pro-tecting minority rights in a multi-ethnic and regionally divided country (Orford, 1997, 454–455; Orford, 2003, 92).

These cases show that it is a mistake to think 'that the choice facing the international community is one between action and inaction', and that it is wrong to imagine 'that the principal threats to peace and security ... emanate from the state or local level' (Orford, 1997, 444). Rather, the very atrocities that elicit calls for us to "do something" stem in part from already existing interventions. Bringing these back into the picture provides us with a richer set of policy alternatives: ending these interventions; changing unfair trade rules; cancelling debt; paying reparation for colonial plunder; eradicating tax havens; placing taxes on financial transactions; and so on. All of these would help replace already existing practices of intervention that systematically take from, and hence work to "under-develop", poorer countries. In so doing, they would help address the everyday atrocity of mass avoidable death. And, in addressing this everyday atrocity, they would also work to create a world less prone to genocide, ethnic cleansing, war crimes and crimes against humanity. Such alternatives take us far beyond a simple dichotomy of acting through military intervention or "standing aside".

Environmental destruction and mass atrocity

Using World Health Organization Data, the Lancet Commission on Pollution and Health (2017) found that pollution currently kills nine million people per year. That is almost 25,000 people per day. This figure is, according to the co-lead of the commission, 'almost certainly an under-estimate, probably by several million' (cited in Carrington, 2017). Low-income and rapidly industrialising countries suffer 92 per cent of pollution-related deaths. Moreover, the World Health Organization estimates that, between 2030 and 2050, climate change will cause approximately 250,000 additional deaths per year: from malnutrition; malaria; diarrhoea; and heat stress (WHO, 2018). The Climate Vulnerability Forum (2010) estimates are even starker: there were 400,000 deaths related to climate change in

2010, the vast majority of which occurred in developing countries. The Monitor's prediction for 2030 is that there will be 530,000 deaths in the developing world alone.

These deaths do not occur naturally. They occur because of human-induced climate change, intimately related as it is to the way in which humans produce, transport and consume food and other goods, depend upon polluting fuels, and so on. The extent to which people in different parts of the world contribute to the carbon emissions that ultimately lead to these deaths is radically unequal. Adjusted for population size, the USA remains the biggest polluter, emitting three times more CO_2 per person than China. India at 1.4 tons and the African continent at 0.9 tons emit substantially less than the world average of 4.5 tons per person (Clark, 2011). But the costs of climate change affect parts of India and Africa particularly heavily. Given that these differential effects also map on to differences in the colour of peoples' skin, it is no wonder that Black Lives Matter protestors suggested that 'the climate crisis is a racist crisis' (Kelbert, 2016). Indeed, 'in the next five years' and beyond, 'the actions of predominately rich white people will cause the deaths of millions of poor black people who have no responsibility for this crisis' (Hallam, 2016). The climate, therefore, is 'the conduit through which the violence of one group is enacted upon another' (Hallam, 2016).[9] This violence may not involve the direct physical killing that so exercises supporters of just war, humanitarian intervention and the R2P. But it is nonetheless present in the structure of our day-to-day existence through the way in which the everyday actions and omissions of people around the world generate radical differences in life chances. If the aim of military intervention is, as Bellamy (2015a, 138) puts it, 'to increase the overall global pool of protection', why is it that the 'pool of protection' here relates only to people who die as a result of direct forms of violence?

Environmental violence should be addressed, first and foremost, as a matter of justice. In addition, reducing the negative impact of humans on the environment may be vital for the prevention of mass atrocities. Ample literature has addressed the link between environmental change and (directly physically) violent conflict, albeit with mixed results.[10] It would be a mistake to think that conflict will inevitably spring up in light of environmentally induced migration or resource scarcity. Scarcity can, after all, result in co-operation (Adano et al., 2012). It is the case, though, that environmental factors can play and have played a role in causing violent conflicts. In Darfur, for instance, conflicts between pastoralists and agriculturalists increased in the context of long-term desertification.[11] For Ban ki-Moon (2007), 'the Darfur conflict began as an ecological crisis, arising at least in part from climate change'. And whilst the Darfur conflict may have emerged in the context of longer-term climactic changes, it serves, ki-Moon suggested, as a warning for what could happen as the effects of human-induced climate change multiply.[12]

Land, food and violent conflict

Between 2005 and 2007 the global price of staple foods rocketed, sparking a food price crisis in late 2007–2008. An estimated 75 million people were driven to hunger and another 125 million to extreme poverty, all while the agribusiness sector achieved record profits (Gürcan, 2014; Holt-Giménez, 2009, 143). Whilst climate change-induced drought did lead to declining production in the build-up to the crisis, placing too much emphasis here would mistakenly assume that the food price crisis resulted from a simple lack of food. Enough food is grown globally to feed 10 billion people (Holt-Giménez et al., 2012). The problem is with the distribution of food: between those who are 'stuffed' in a world suffering from increasing levels of obesity and those who are 'starved' (Patel, 2008); between places where food is systematically wasted and places where food is sorely needed; and between companies and investors who hoard food in the hope that prices keep increasing and people who need it immediately (Clapp and Helleiner, 2012).

The food crisis is intimately linked to the wider global injustices discussed in the first section of this chapter, and to policy measures at national, regional and global levels which prioritise mechanised, large-scale agriculture over small-scale and often environmentally friendly farming (see, e.g., Dunford, 2016, 13–42). SAPs, discussed above, called for cuts to agricultural supports on which rural people depended. As the World Bank (2007, 138) later admitted, 'structural adjustment in the 1980s' thereby 'dismantled the elaborate system of public agencies that provided farmers with access to land, credit, insurance, inputs and cooperative organisation'. SAPs also demanded that countries open up to free trade. With large and often heavily subsidised farms in Europe and the USA producing staple foods extremely cheaply – albeit with huge externalised environmental costs in terms of soil depletion, pollution and high water use – free trade in food made it extremely difficult for small-scale producers in the global South to compete. Imported food was available in local markets in the global South at a price lower than the domestic cost of production. Many farmers in the South, unable to compete with cheap, imported food, were 'driven off their land into deepening poverty' (Martínez-Torres and Rosset, 2010, 162). To give an example, 'conservative UN Food and Agriculture Organization estimates suggest that upwards of 30 million peasants lost their land' in the first 'decade after the World Trade Organization was established' (McMichael, 2009, 154).[13] Many of the farmers who did not lose their land had little option but to produce single crops – cocoa, coffee, farmed fish – to export to consumers in the global North (Pritchard, 2009).

From such changes emerged the global food regime that we see today. Staple grains are produced *en masse* through mechanised forms of production that degrade soil and depend upon the use of highly polluting inputs. They are then shipped around the world, perhaps to feed growing numbers of industrially farmed animals, perhaps to be turned into sugars that make some processed foods palatable, perhaps to be turned into the plastic and cardboard packaged cereal we find in supermarkets and convenience stores. Meanwhile, 'across the developing world, land and resources', rather than being used to provide a rich and varied diet for local people, are used 'for integrated, export-oriented agri-food investments' (Pritchard, 2009, 301). Not only does this system exacerbate the environmental problems mentioned above – some United Nations (UN) estimates suggest that the global food system, when inputs and transport are included, contributes to around half of global carbon emissions (Sangheri, 2016). It also generates huge vulnerability in the face of changing food prices. When the price of food rises – due to climate change-induced reduction in supply or, given the dependence of the global food regime on fuel, due to fluctuating oil prices – millions of people are plunged into hunger (Gürcan, 2014).

Far from witnessing a shift to providing support for local food producers, the aftermath of the food crisis has seen an intensification of the very dynamics – of the dispossession of rural people and of agricultural concentration – that helped create the crisis in the first place. Knowing that land is likely to increase in value, investors, including pension funds investing the money of millions of "ordinary" people, targeted land as a safe bet for investment after previously reliable financial instruments imploded in 2007–2008. At the same time some states – having seen food prices play a key role in Arab Spring uprisings and fearful that "food insecurity" could lead to insurrection – leased land abroad on a long-term basis to mass-produce food in order to feed their domestic population (Liberti, 2013). Simultaneously, desire for land to grow biofuels and to meet carbon offsetting targets also increased interest in land (Fairhead et al., 2012; Kelly, 2011). This confluence of factors resulted in a huge increase in large-scale land deals – deals in which swathes of land are sold to investors or leased on a very long-term basis, often for the purpose of export-oriented production. Initial World Bank estimates were frightening: before 2008, around four million hectares of cultivable or cultivated land were transferred per year, while from October 2008 to August 2009 alone, more than 45 million hectares were traded (Deininger et al., 2011, xiv). Whilst these early estimates are now considered too high – in part because social movement and civil society activism helped ensure that deals often involved smaller quantities of land than initially planned – the latest data suggest that large-scale land deals continue to be an important and significant trend globally, particularly in sub-Saharan Africa (Nolte et al., 2016). The Land Matrix database, which includes only international investment in land and does not claim to capture all such deals, records 1,204 concluded deals which cover over 42.2 million hectares of land – an area three times the size of England. Intended deals target a further 20 million hectares (Nolte et al., 2016).

Despite being accompanied by narratives of 'underused' and 'underutilized' land, small-scale farmers, pastoralists and indigenous peoples depend for their livelihoods on access to and food from the land taken (World Bank, 2009, 2; 50; Peters, 2013). And yet, in only about 14 per cent of the deals documented by the Land Matrix has a process of free, prior and informed consent been conducted. Only 43 per cent have involved any process of consultation, however (in)adequate. Land deals are also reported to involve extensive rights violations and have a negative impact on already marginalised rural people, driving them into hunger and poverty (see, e.g., De Schutter, 2011). The lack of transparency around land deals makes it impossible to get an overall sense of the amount of people displaced, or indeed of the extent of rights violations that these deals involve (Cotula, 2014). What is clear, though, is that numerous academic and civil society reports, including reports from the UN Special Rapporteur on the Right to Food, indicate that displacement and rights violations are rife. Reports in Cambodia (Global

Witness, 2013), Cameroon (Oakland Institute, 2012), Ethiopia (Oakland Institute, 2014), Ghana (Tsikata and Yaro, 2014), Laos (Global Witness, 2013), Mali (Oakland Institute, 2011), Mozambique (Nhantumbo and Salomão, 2010; Sabaratnam, 2017), Sierra Leone (Millar, 2016), Uganda (Oxfam, 2011) and Tanzania (Twomey et al., 2015) have all highlighted extensive displacement and rights violations. Women have been particularly affected, given that they often do not have formal rights to land and are hence even less likely to be involved in consultations or to receive compensation (Doss et al., 2014). In light of the lack of adequate consultation and resulting displacement and rights violations, some refer to large-scale land acquisitions as a global land grab and a 'new colonialism' (Liberti, 2013).

Land grabs involve a complex array of actors, both national and transnational. Land Matrix, which is focused on international investments, notes that the top five countries of origin of investors fuelling land deals are Malaysia, the USA, the UK (not including Jersey and other UK-associated tax havens, which are also heavily represented), Singapore and Saudi Arabia (Nolte et al., 2016). Investors often come from private companies (40 per cent of concluded deals) and stock exchange listed firms (an additional 30 per cent). They are supported, though, by states and development organisations. Governments in target countries have offered land for lease at extremely cheap rates, though only 15.4 per cent of deals concluded since the year 2000 include a domestic shareholder (Nolte et al., 2016). Foreign governments have also supported large-scale land deals through their development initiatives. G7 country governments, for instance, supported the New Alliance for Food Security and Nutrition – a public–private partnership aiming to drive agricultural investment through the creation of large farms.[14] The New Alliance has been given lots of financial support by the UK Department for International Development, United States Agency for International Development, a series of donors including the Gates Foundation, and a number of agribusiness companies including Monsanto and Cargill. The Alliance was later condemned by the European Parliament for failing to consult locally and for supporting investments that 'result in serious human rights violations' (EU Parliament, 2016, 9). Despite this condemnation, a wide range of donors continue to support it. The continuing prevalence of large-scale land deals shows that international actors are already intervening, reproducing an agricultural model which generates dependence on food imports, contributes enormously to environmental destruction and results in the dispossession of small farmers, driving many into hunger, poverty and suicide.

In addition to being important in its own right, the cessation of land grabbing is also vital if we want to take seriously the prevention of the mass atrocities considered under the narrow remit of the R2P. To date, research on whether the recent wave of large-scale land acquisitions has increased the likelihood of violent conflict has been minimal. Nonetheless, even before the new wave of land deals are taken into consideration, 'local conflicts over land and territory' have 'increasingly' been 'recognised as important bottom-up drivers of protracted, destructive and traumatic wars' (Boone, 2014, 327), including wars in the Democratic Republic of Congo (Huggins et al., 2005), Darfur (Flint, 2009; Abdul-Jalil and Unruh, 2013), South Sudan (Justin and van Leeuwen, 2016), Rwanda (Bigagaza et al., 2002), Sierra Leone and Liberia. Indeed, the UN Interagency Framework Team for Preventive Action (2012) found that land issues had played a significant role in all but three of more than 30 intra-state conflicts taking place in Africa – the continent most targeted for large-scale land acquisitions – since 1990.[15] Not only do land issues drive violent conflict. They also sustain it: land is taken as a spoil of war, as occurred in Darfur when Janjaweed and other militias kept land that they had cleared through ethnic cleansing; and lack of clarity over who owns land when people have fled from it during conflict makes peace settlements difficult to reach and maintain.

That there are so many cases in which land has been an underlying driver of conflict and a resource that sustains war ought to give those concerned with mass atrocity prevention reason to be worried about the implications of land grabs. If land played such a key role even before the occurrence of a new wave of land acquisitions in Africa, what will happen as vast swathes of land on which people depend are being enclosed? Early signs suggest that land deals are resulting in direct physical violence. After being left without access to water following the establishment of a new 31,000-acre plantation near Koka in southwest Ethiopia, Suri people took up arms against government forces, who later retaliated and killed 54 unarmed Suri in a market place. More broadly, the establishment of the plantation 'dramatically disturbed the delicate political order between ethnic groups in the region by upsetting historically established grazing practices and exacerbating pre-existing ethnic tensions' (Oakland Institute, 2014, 5). When people are displaced, they lose access to water and other vital resources and are hence forced to move to other land, which potentially results in conflict with existing land-users. Moreover, ethnographic research conducted at locations affected by a 40,000-hectare bio-energy project in the rural north of Sierra Leone – a country still recovering from a deadly civil war that raged through the 1990s – reveals 'increasing social tensions', with many people considering 'violence against the company a very real possibility' (Millar, 2016, 570; 575).[16]

When land – so often a factor in starting, sustaining or resuming conflict – is being grabbed at an alarming rate, it is little wonder that the UN Interagency Framework Team for Preventive Action (2012, 1) reports that the 'mismanagement of land and natural resources is contributing to new conflicts and obstructing the peaceful transition of existing ones'. And yet, consideration of international investments in land, together with consideration of environmental change and global injustice more broadly, are entirely absent from the R2P framework, focused as it is on internal drivers of conflict. With the complicity of international actors – including governments, investors, businesses and ordinary pension holders whose money may be going into land – ignored, so too are actions that would make a real difference in preventing future war crimes, ethnic cleansing, genocide and crimes against humanity. The governments and development agencies currently investing in land acquisitions could "do something" by implementing legislative changes that would halt the global land grab and, where appropriate and desired by potential recipients, by redirecting their money and energy towards support for small-scale farmers, pastoralists and indigenous peoples. Until they cease to facilitate violent land grabs, it is hard to take seriously the notion that such actors are fit for the purpose of protecting others through military means; a point we shall elaborate upon in the following chapter.

Stoking ethnic tensions

Calls for humanitarian military intervention in the 1990s arose in response to a perceived rise in ethnic conflict. For Tom Farer (1996, 15), different ethnic groups are 'likely to go on clawing at each other unless external actors' intervene in order to 'either club them into submission [or] break the stalemate'. His bombastic remarks were not uncommon. 'Many security texts' suggested 'that irrational "ethnic particularism" or religious tensions' were 'emerging as major threats to peace and security' (Orford, 2003, 173). Today, concerns over Islamist extremism and conflict in the Middle East are articulated as concerns over sectarian conflict. Such accounts ignore the role that international actors play in stoking ethnic and sectarian tensions.

This role was and still is particularly visible in areas most recently subjected to European colonial rule. In sub-Saharan Africa, European colonial powers claimed ownership or trusteeship of all land even when they could not exert direct rule over vast swathes of it. To maintain ownership and control, colonial administrators between 1910 and 1940 cemented 'alliances with selected rural strongmen – chiefs, emirs, kings, elders and other local rulers – who could serve as their agents or partners in ruling the countryside' (Boone, 2014, 27). With the help of anthropologists who did research aimed at 'defining, delineating, or creating the "natural tribal communities" that were presumed to be the authentic African social form', colonial authorities delimited territorial jurisdictions (Boone, 2014, 26). In some cases, ethnic, tribal and geographically defined groups were 'invented of whole cloth by colonial governors', while in others they bore only 'very limited resemblance to pre-colonial land rules and practices' (Boone, 2014, 25). In assigning 'subject populations to rulers and territories', often on ethnic grounds, these divisions served to "containerise" African populations by splitting them into a range of separate, sometimes conflicting, ethnic cages (Boone, 2014, 29; Mamdani, 1996). Moreover, designated (neo-)customary rulers were 'invested with wide-ranging executive and judicial authority to exercise within their official territorial domains' (Boone, 2014, 27). They had power to distribute land and other resources to "their" people and responsibilities to gather resources to give to their colonial masters. They exercised these responsibilities by introducing 'a whole range of compulsions' including 'forced labour, forced crops, forced sales, forced contributions, and forced removals' (Mamdani, 1996, 23). Being part of certain groups would, then, bring benefits, whilst being part of others would bring additional compulsions. Policing the boundaries of such groups thus became increasingly important, and previously fluid (or indeed non-existent) distinctions were magnified and fixed into place.

These distinctions and divisions have played a role in recent conflict in sub-Saharan Africa. The Rwandan genocide – an attempt, led by Hutu elites, to eliminate the entire Tutsi population – is a case in point. Whilst the Hutu–Tutsi distinction did exist prior to colonial rule, it was far from a fixed division. Hutus and Tutsis lived together in villages. They married one another, and shared a religion, language and territory. That such a fluid distinction should lie at the heart of genocidal killing requires some explanation. This explanation centres around the ways in which colonial rule turned a fluid distinction into an increasingly fixed and antagonistic one.

Rwanda was ruled by Belgium under a League of Nations mandate between 1916 and 1945, having previously been part of German East Africa since the late 19th century. Missionaries who visited Rwanda regarded Tutsis, in Menard's (cited in Mamdani, 2002, 88) words, as 'a European under a black skin'. Rwandan society was read through a worldview according to which Africa was a place with no civilisation. 'Every sign of "progress" on the dark continent was … taken as evidence of a civilizing influence of an outsider race' (Mamdani, 2002, 79). Members of this "outsider race" were deemed 'Caucasians who were black in colour without being negroid in race'. Through this hypothesis was 'born the Hamites of Africa, separated from the Bantu, so-called real Africans' (Mamdani, 2002, 79). The colonial state thus identified 'Hutu as indigenous and Tutsi as Alien' (Mamdani, 2002, 34).

This imagined racial difference between Hamite Tutsis and Bantu Hutus was then written into the institutions of colonial rule (Mamdani, 2002, 88). The colonisers provided education for Tutsis and set them up as client elites who would rule over, and extract wealth from, Hutus.[17] State administration was changed; powers that had previously been split – albeit unevenly – between Hutu chiefs of the land, Tutsi chiefs of the pastures and Tutsi chiefs of the men were fused into a single role. Hutus were thus removed from power and different authorities were replaced with a single chief able to exercise unfettered control over people in a given area. Finally, uneven taxes were applied. Hutus were subject to *Ubureetwa* – a particularly harsh form of labour in which they were forced to provide labour in return for access to land provided by Tutsi chiefs. The Tutsi chiefs were, in turn, ruled by colonial masters and effectively forced to extract resources from Hutus. According to elderly Tutsi refugees in Uganda, the Belgian attitude was that 'you whip the Hutu or we whip you' (cited in Watson, 1991, 4). Rather than fostering solidarity against colonial rule, these practices magnified divisions, with Tutsi rulers also able to profit through 'extra-legal exactions' from Hutus (Mamdani, 2002, 97). After these perceived racial differences were given institutional form, they were entrenched in formal, legal identities – later used in the genocide to determine who should be killed – through a census in 1933–1934 which classified the entire Rwandan population as Hutu, Tutsi or Twa. Belgian power thus racialised a previously socio-political distinction, creating the fixed division that went on to lie at the heart of genocidal killing.

Our purpose here is not to give a comprehensive account of why the Rwandan genocide took place, but to illustrate the way in which international attempts to stoke ethnic tensions create conditions in which atrocity is more likely to occur. This point can also be illustrated in relation to the Syrian civil war; the war that, in George Osborne's words, highlights the price of *not* intervening. Divide and rule was a policy of French colonial rule in Syria post-World War One, and sectarianism continued to be politically mobilised under the post-colonial rule of Hafez Assad and Bashar al-Assad (Fildis, 2011). It has also been internationally stoked following the deposition of Saddam Hussein – a Sunni ruler – after the 2003 war in Shia-majority Iraq. In light of the post-war emergence of a Shia government in Iraq, Saudi Arabia and Jordan were concerned about the rise of a Shia "crescent" across the Middle East, with Iran governed by Shia leaders and Syria governed by the minority Alawite sect of Shia Islam. Regional media sources – mostly indirectly owned by the Saudis and other gulf states – also amplified growing tensions, as did actors from beyond the region (Phillips, 2015). WikiLeaks cables reveal that regime change in

Syria has been desired by the US government from at least 2006 and that stoking ethnic tension has been considered as a strategy for undermining the Assad regime. A December 2006 WikiLeaks cable authored by William Roebuck, then chargé d'affaires at the US embassy in Damascus, calls for undermining the Syrian government 'by any available means' (in Naiman, 2015, 290). The cable – one of many written by several people – recommends that the USA

> play on Sunni fears of Iranian influence. There are fears in Syria that the Iranians are active in both Shia proselytizing and conversion of, mostly poor, Sunnis. Though often exaggerated, such fears reflect an element of the Sunni community in Syria that is increasingly upset by and focused on the spread of Iranian influence in their country.[18]

The strategy, here, is one of fanning the flames of sectarian tension. Extraordinarily, this cable was written at the height of Sunni–Shia fighting in Iraq. There is no way that the US government and the author of this cable could have been unaware of the dangerous implications of seeking to incite Sunni–Shia sectarianism. There is also no indication that this is an exception or the product of a rogue member of staff: Roebuck was on good standing and went on to serve the US embassies in Iraq and Libya (Naiman, 2015).

Such tactics are also discussed explicitly in a US army funded RAND report, which identifies divide and rule as a potential strategy for the USA in the Middle East. The report (Pernin et al., 2008, xvi) suggests that US leaders could use 'covert action, information operations, unconventional warfare' and other means to 'capitalise on the sustained Shia–Sunni conflict trajectory by taking the side of the conservative Sunni regimes against Shiite empowerment in the Muslim world ... possibly supporting Sunni governments against a continuingly hostile Iran'.[19] These and related strategies have been adopted, with support given to opponents of the regime and funding provided to citizen journalists exposing the barbarism of the regime – both later acknowledged by the US government (see, e.g., Allday, 2016).[20] To be clear, such strategies are not exclusively responsible for the outbreak of conflict in Syria. Ethnographic research conducted in 2007–2010 suggests that most Syrians didn't outwardly project sectarianism, despite the attempts by an array of actors to stoke such tensions (Phillips, 2015). These tensions did, however, come to the fore when Arab Spring protests were violently repressed by Bashar al-Assad, and they have played a key role in the descent of the conflict into an increasingly sectarian war.

International involvement has magnified since the outbreak of conflict in Syria. Through the Central Intelligence Agency (CIA) and in cooperation with Saudi Arabia amongst others, the USA have been attempting to train and equip Syrian rebels since 2013. They have 'trained and equipped nearly 10,000 fighters sent into Syria' (Higgins, 2015). The USA, together with regional allies and later joined by the UK and France, have also been bombing targets in northern Syria since September 2014. Of course, harmful intervention is not only a Western phenomenon. The Turkish government turned 'a blind eye' to the destination of 'funds, arms and fighters crossing the Turkish border' and flowing to extremist groups like al-Qaeda affiliated Jabhat al-Nusra, and Saudi Arabia approved the formation of openly anti-Alawi groups (Phillips, 2015, 370). Indeed, the flow of cash, often raised by private citizens and charities for sectarian militias, has encouraged militias to amplify their sectarian rhetoric in order to attract support. And this is before we get to the devastating Russian bombs or to the Iranian military support for the Assad regime. The notion that the international community is sitting on the sidelines in Syria is thus 'fundamentally false'. Amongst other things, it 'ignores several years of the West and its regional allies (primarily Turkey, Saudi Arabia and Qatar) arming, funding and training rebel groups, the crippling economic sanctions imposed against the Syrian government, ongoing airstrikes, special forces operations, and a host of other diplomatic, military and economic measures' (Allday, 2016; see also Bâli and Rana, 2017).

In the context of such already existing interventions, George Osborne's claim (in Wintour, 2016a) that the crisis in Syria emerged out of a 'vacuum of Western leadership' and reflects 'the price of non-intervention' falls apart. So, too, does the argument that Syria retrospectively shows that the disaster in Libya has been vindicated. The crisis in Syria has a lot to do with the vicious suppression of pro-democracy protests. But it also has a lot to do with a whole host of interventions, from attempts to ferment sectarian divides to the provision of funds, weapons, training and troops. When we reject the misleading choice between "intervening" and "standing aside", other options start to appear. As a long-term move, we might pressure governments and media sources to *stop* fuelling sectarian division. We might learn lessons from past interventions that have generated the massive regional instability that makes parts of the Middle East so difficult to govern today. In the shorter term, we might call on parties to the conflict to withdraw Special Forces and proxy troops. We might call for a full and fully enforced arms embargo. We might call for 'real diplomacy for ending war, not fake diplomacy designed to enable joint bombing campaigns' (Bennis, 2016). And we might call for meaningful attempts to protect refugees (see, e.g., Souter, 2016).

Providing the spark: the arms trade

Missiles raining down one day, new kit for a bombed-out
hospital the next. Such is the UK's warped Yemen policy.
(Mohamed, Yemen Researcher for Amnesty International, 2017)

In 2015, global military spending totalled $1,676 billion. That is nearly $250 for each and every one of the earth's seven billion people (Holden et al., 2016, 1). The conventional arms industry has also been growing: 2017 saw the highest levels of spending on conventional weapons since the Cold War era (Dehghan, 2017). The small arms trade has grown threefold in the past 15 years – the years in which states have, according to R2P supporters, expressed their commitment to protect civilians. There are now at least 800 million small arms and light weapons in circulation (UN, 2015b). Entrenched conflict in North Africa and the Middle East has not led to any reduction in small arms transfers and has occurred alongside a near doubling of conventional weapons sales to the region (Small Arms Survey, 2015, 114; Dehghan, 2017). Trade in conventional weapons is dominated by the permanent five members of the UN Security Council (China, Russia, the USA, the UK and France). The trade, though, is global; finding a country that is not deeply integrated into networks of arms trading is very difficult, save for countries that are placed under often ineffective sanctions. Indeed, researchers at the University of British Columbia identified 502 violations of UN arms embargoes, finding that only two resulted in any legal action whatsoever and only one in a conviction (Parliament, 2012). All of this in an industry that is heavily subsidised and riddled with 'endemic and systematic' corruption. Indeed, the arms industry is 'arguably one of the most – if not *the most* – corrupt industries in the world' (Holden et al., 2016, 118).

Even a small redirection of the money spent on arms could make a marked difference to the scale of everyday atrocity. But the arms trade is not only a problem because it uses resources that could improve living conditions for millions of people. It also plays a role in reproducing a world in which directly physically violent events that shock the conscience of humankind continue to occur. Access to weapons is vital for regimes that use oppression to remain in power. And in case the reader thinks that states – particularly "liberal" ones – are reluctant to provide arms to dictatorial regimes: when it comes to conventional arms, 'Western (European and US) arms sales do not systematically prefer democracies', and the USA even seems 'to prefer more autocratic regimes' (De Soysa and Midford, 2012, 844). The UK government identified 28 countries of concern in a 2014–2015 human rights and democracy report only to approve arms export licences to 18 of them (CAAT, 2017). Similar findings hold regarding the relationship between arms sales and human rights: European powers do not favour human rights-respecting regimes when transferring arms (Perkins and Neumayer, 2010). 'Western foreign policy rhetoric' therefore 'does not match reality' (De Soysa and Midford, 2012, 844).

Even if states were more selective in granting arms export licences, they would still have little control over where exported weapons end up. As we saw in the first chapter on Libya, weapons stocks moved rapidly across borders to arm insurgencies in Mali and Somalia, and to arm Islamic State and al-Qaeda affiliates. Moreover, it is always hard to tell what weapons will be used for in the future. Situations in which interveners fight against the weapons that they themselves provided are common, occurring recently in Libya and in the fight against Islamic State across North Africa and the Middle East. Between 2003 and 2014, for instance, the post-Saddam Hussein Iraqi regime received weapons worth $4.115 billion (Holden et al., 2016, 61).[21] Stacks of these weapons were subsequently acquired by Islamic State. In June 2014 alone, they obtained enough weapons to arm and equip more than three Iraqi conventional army divisions. More broadly, Islamic State used ammunition from at least 21 different countries, manufactured over the course of 70 years. Nearly 20 per cent of that ammunition was supplied by the USA (Conflict Armament Research, 2014). When we hear about "zones of barbarism" and "zones of civility", we should remember that these zones are already tied together through the transfer of weaponry. The provision of weapons from the supposedly separate "zones of civility" facilitates the very "barbarism" that elicits pleas for action.

As genocide unfolded in Rwanda, the international community "stood aside" to watch weapons provided by some of its members get turned on civilians. The Rwandan genocide is remembered for the sheer extent of participation in killing, with some people using machetes, ordinarily used for farming, as a weapon of war. The largest massacres, though, were carried out with heavy weaponry during military operations. Such weaponry was 'almost all purchased in the four years leading up to the genocide' (Holden et al., 2016, 75). Between 1990 and 1994, in the context of war with the Rwandan Patriotic Front, the Rwandan state spent 70 per cent of its budget – including some of the loans it received from the World Bank – on arms (Melvern, 2006, 57). The biggest supplier by far was France. The international community may have been bystanders as the genocide took place, but they were not bystanders when it came to providing the weapons with which it was carried out.

Similarly, in Libya the North Atlantic Treaty Organization (NATO) intervened in order to fight against weapons that its very own members had provided. When a European Union embargo on arms sales to Libya was lifted in 2004, then UK foreign secretary Jack Straw said it was 'a very good day … for peace and security across the world' (cited in BBC, 2004). European Union arms sales to Libya increased year on year afterwards, with €343.7 million worth sold to Libya in 2009 (*The Guardian*, 2011). Italy were by far the largest exporter, with France a distant second, although the UK increased their exports tenfold the following year, issuing licences for £216 million worth of military equipment. On 27 January 2011, shortly before Resolution 1973 authorising military intervention was agreed, the UK signed off a licence for the unlimited export of military communications equipment (CAAT, 2013). Less than two months later, NATO were dropping bombs to destroy stocks of the munitions that their own members had been supplying. Arms sales to a still fragile Libya resumed just a year later with Gerard Howarth, former UK Junior Defence Minister, saying that 'we liberated the Iraqis from a tyrant, we liberated Libya from a tyrant, frankly, I want to see UK business benefit from the liberation we give to their people' (cited in Stearman, 2011).

Arms sales that facilitate mass atrocities continue as we write, with the UK and the USA selling weapons that are being used on Yemeni civilians. In March 2015 a coalition led by Saudi Arabia and consisting of members of the Gulf Cooperation Council (excluding Oman), Egypt, Jordan, Morocco, Pakistan and Sudan began a bombing campaign against Houthi rebels in Yemen in support of the government of Abdrabbuh Hadi.[22] In January 2017, just under two years after the start of the bombing campaign, UN Humanitarian Coordinator for Yemen Jamie McGolddrick (cited in al-Haj, 2017) said that 'over 10,000 people have been killed' and 'almost 40,000 people injured'. The 'large majority' of these deaths have been caused by coalition air strikes (Wearing, 2016, 5). As of August 2017, nearly 19 million people – 80 per cent of the population – are in need of humanitarian aid, 16 million lack access to water or sanitation and 17 million are hungry, with nearly seven million facing famine (UN News, 2017).

Human Rights Watch (2016; 2017) have reported in detail a series of war crimes committed since the start of the intervention, including attacks on marketplaces – some using US bombs – and attacks on residential compounds (Human Rights Watch, 2016). On 19 April 2015, the coalition bombed an Oxfam warehouse containing humanitarian aid (Wearing, 2016, 10). Then UN Humanitarian Coordinator for Yemen, Johannes van der Klaauw (2015), responded to these attacks by saying that 'the indiscriminate bombing of populated areas, with or without prior warning, is in contravention of international humanitarian law'. The attacks nonetheless continued, with the coalition dropping bombs on a Médicins Sans Frontières hospital even though the name and logo of the hospital was printed on the roof and the coalition had been provided with the hospital's coordinates (Wearing, 2016, 10).

Despite these widespread allegations of war crimes, the UK and the USA are still providing logistical and technical support for the campaign and selling arms to Saudi Arabia. In 2016, then UK Prime Minister David Cameron (cited in Osbourne, 2016) said that the UK 'have the strictest rules for arms exports of almost any country anywhere in the world'. The British government claims that its arms control regulations exceed the requirements of the UN Arms Trade Treaty, which entered into force in late 2014. And yet, despite widespread condemnation, the UK government continues to provide weapons that are being used – illegally – on Yemeni civilians (Wearing, 2016); a fact that justifies scepticism about whether the arms trade treaty will make a real difference in regulating the arms trade.[23] In the two years after the start of the intervention, the UK approved 194 export licences for arms and related equipment to Saudi Arabia. Collectively, these licences were worth more than £3.3 billion (Rights Watch UK, 2017). This is around 10 times the value of aid sent to Yemen by the UK and USA combined. New reports released at the time of writing this chapter in September 2017 suggest that UK Weapons companies have made £6 billion from Saudi Arabia since the start of the coalition bombing campaign (Dearden, 2017). UK arms sales to Saudi Arabia have been met with widespread condemnation from, amongst others, Save the Children, Amnesty International, Human Rights Watch, the House of Commons International Development Committee and a range of UK political parties (Wearing, 2016). They have also been condemned by then UN Secretary-General Ban ki-Moon (cited in Wintour, 2016b), who upon visiting London in February 2016 said that 'we need states that are party to the arms treaty to set an example in fulfilling one of the treaty's main purposes – controlling arms flows to actors that may use them in ways that breach international humanitarian law'.

♦ ♦ ♦

The arms trade together with the production of "underdevelopment", environmental violence, land grabbing and attempts to stoke ethnic tension show that the international community, far from being a passive bystander, already intervenes in a manner that reproduces a structurally violent world. Moreover, it would be a mistake to think of everyday killing and the four mass atrocity crimes to which the R2P responds as separate issues, to be addressed in different policy circles and in different academic debates. For the international interventions that result in the atrocity of mass avoidable death also create conditions that are conducive to the emergence of these atrocity crimes. The very agents that are called upon to save people through military intervention are already implicated in the killing. In the next chapter, we argue that, rather than calling for military interventions by actors that sell arms, facilitate land grabs, enact environmental violence and stoke ethnic tension, we should call for an end to these structural forms of violence. Only such a politics is fit for the purpose of tackling everyday atrocity and, in the process, creating a world less conducive to genocide, war crimes, ethnic cleansing and crimes against humanity.

5 | JUST WAR AND THE RESPONSIBILITY TO PROTECT IN A WORLD OF ALREADY EXISTING INTERVENTION

So far, we have shown that contemporary just war thinking and the Responsibility to Protect (R2P) fail to address the realities of the wars that they call for. They also delete from the picture already existing interventions and therefore follow George Osborne (in Wintour, 2016a) in imagining that humanitarian crises emerge in 'a vacuum'. Our previous chapter blew open this narrow and distorting framework. We showed that humanitarian crises do not emerge in a vacuum. They emerge in part through the actions and omissions of the so-called international community. This means that the repertoire of possible international action in preventing and responding to mass atrocities is far more extensive than imagined in just war thinking and the R2P. Concerned international actors have a choice that escapes the binary of either saving lives through military intervention or passively standing aside. In place of other-defending war and beyond the limited repertoire of norm dissemination, capacity building and preventative diplomacy suggested in the R2P are a whole range of possible measures including:[1] cessation of arms sales; simple, affordable health interventions that prevent avoidable child deaths; debt cancellation; protection of customary land rights; and attempts to challenge both environmental destruction and the forms of aid in reverse that condemn parts of the world to poverty and hunger.

What are the implications of focusing on the realities of humanitarian war, already existing intervention and everyday atrocity? Is it the case that just war thinking and the R2P are 'insufficient' and 'incomplete': that in order to improve atrocity prevention, we need to *add* to an otherwise unchanged framework a focus on intervention that is already taking place (Brown and Bohm, 2016, 897)?[2] Or are the implications more radical? In this chapter, we argue that they are, and that we should reject the R2P and other-defending wars in favour of non-militarist alternatives. First, we claim that actors already engaged in damaging practices of intervention are not fit for the purpose of other-defending *military* intervention. Second, we argue that the idea of a just war and the R2P norm both legitimise a moralistic form of militarism. They contribute to a moral climate characterised by the dangerous misperception that militarism is an appropriate and just response to mass atrocity.

Far from offering protection against excessive violence and simultaneously being the vanguard of a progressive change towards a less violent world, the R2P is a dangerous norm that is not fit for purpose. Far from preventing and responding appropriately to mass atrocities, it gives a veneer of legitimacy to military interventions performed by states that are already engaged in damaging forms of political and economic intervention, while also occluding the wider changes that are required in order to create a world in which we can say "no more Rwandas" and truly mean it.

Bad international citizenship

Much as people can be good citizens by way of contributing to the life of their political community, states are able to be good citizens by way of contributing to the life of the international community (Wheeler and Dunne, 1998). The debate on good international citizenship in the context of mass atrocity reflects, however, the narrow framework of the R2P (Souter, 2016). States are considered able to act well as part of an international society that is increasingly intolerant of mass atrocities through norm dissemination, preventative diplomacy and, as a last resort, military intervention. This ignores ways of embodying good international citizenship that go beyond the limited toolbox provided by the R2P. States might, for instance, contribute to a society in which people are protected by taking in and supporting refugees fleeing mass atrocity crimes (Souter, 2016). Or, to draw on our previous chapters, they might act well by providing additional resources for those 'simple and affordable' health interventions that would prevent the majority of the nearly six million deaths of children under five that take place each year (WHO, 2017a). States that fail to do these things are bad international citizens. They act badly in other ways too: by blocking attempts to prevent refugees from drowning in the Mediterranean Sea; by selling arms that are used on civilians; and by contributing to the environmental destruction that is both a killer in its own right and a potential driver of future atrocity crimes.

Does expanding the remit of what states can do to be good international citizens mean that they should continue to intervene militarily but *also* demonstrate their commitment to protecting people through other means (see, e.g., Souter, 2016)? No. If states are not demonstrating their willingness to protect people in general, then why should they be called upon to protect them through means of violence? If states are keeping refugees – who arrive after a long and arduous journey – in detention centres where their rights are frequently violated, what reason do we have to think that they will protect people responsibly when they do so using military means? Bad international citizens are *not fit* for the purpose of humanitarian military intervention.[3]

Proponents of just war and the R2P disagree. They insist that we must take seriously the interests that govern world politics. States have a track record of acting in the name of partial interests, whether a perceived "national" interest or the interests of a select group of people and/or corporations. Since we cannot wish such interests away, we must try to work with them. This will lead to a great deal of inconsistency: states might protect people in Kosovo out of an interest in stemming migration or providing reason for the continued existence of the North Atlantic Treaty Organization (NATO), but "stand aside" in Rwanda. They might call for military protection in Syria, but continue to sell arms that are used on Yemeni civilians out of an interest in maintaining strong relations with Saudi Arabia and supporting a strong arms industry. They might – as Russia did – call for authorisation under the R2P for military protection in South Ossetia, only to then facilitate further oppression in Syria in order to maintain an overseas naval base, access to the Mediterranean Sea and influence in the Middle East more broadly. Or they might make noises around intervention in Darfur, but continue to cause environmental harms that are expected to be at the heart of numerous Darfur-like conflicts in the future. This inconsistency and 'hypocrisy', Dunne and Gelber (2015, 227) point out, 'is a long-standing feature of the sovereignty-based order'. But it need not be a problem: 'strategic interests sometimes do align with humanitarian concerns and this is not necessarily a bad thing. The international community cannot be expected to be present in all cases. Prudential considerations do come into play when decisions are made' (Sahnoun, 2011, 477).[4] Indeed, just war theorist Brian Orend (2013, 99) goes as far as to say that 'it is indefensible to suggest that failure to have intervened in one spot ... implies that for the sake of some twisted concern for consistency we should fail to intervene everywhere else'. According to this view, states may contribute to humanitarian outcomes even if the 'motivations [they] have for supporting R2P may be driven by interests that have little or nothing to do with responsible sovereignty' (Dunne and Gelber, 2015, 227).

This view makes the mistake of treating national interests as 'relatively innocuous' – as preserving stability, increasing trade and stemming the tide of refugees (Graubart 2013, 78). It fails to recognise that the interests and moral character of states shape their decisions to intervene and undermine the very possibility of interventions being humanitarian and protective.

What are the interests of, for instance, the USA and the UK? Our choice of these states is informed not by their levels of culpability – numerous states are guilty of failures to address everyday atrocity. Rather, it is informed by the role that they played in interventions in Kosovo and Libya; interventions which were considered, respectively, to have revealed a need for a new norm of protection and to have shown this new norm working 'exactly as it was supposed to' (Evans, 2012). Accounting for what the interests of the USA and the UK are is difficult, not least because such interests are multiple, complex and contested. What is clear from the last chapter, though, is that these states have been facilitating the global land grab, sell vast amounts of weapons and are amongst the highest polluters. In the case of the USA, they have also withdrawn from a landmark international climate change agreement. We also know that a Pentagon-sponsored bipartisan task force report from 2000 lists as reasons to use force not only the prevention of genocide but also 'the prevention of any rival hegemon or coalition, access to vital resources, and extension of global economic integration along market-friendly lines' (Graubart, 2013, 78; USCNS, 2000). This is not just a matter of the choice of particular US leaders. It is an institutionalised foreign policy. We know, moreover, that UK Junior Minister Robert Howarth (cited in BBC, 2011b) said with reference to arms sales to post-war Libya and Iraq that 'we liberated the Iraqis from a tyrant, we liberated Libya from a tyrant, frankly, I want to see UK business benefit from the liberation we give to their people'. These stated interests have been furthered through action: the renewal of arms sales to an unstable Libya mere months after the "end" of the civil war and a massive US military projection that includes 'expanding US military bases, and setting up regional unified command facilities for each part of the world' (Graubart, 2013, 78).

Why do these interests render interventions inhumanitarian and unprotective? Take Kosovo. The USA showed minimal interest in the Rambouillet talks – held when there were real hopes of a peace deal in early 1999. They also offered minimal condemnation of war crimes carried out by Kosovars under the cover of NATO air support. Such conduct cannot be explained with reference to humanitarian protection. If we instead think of the mission as giving a renewed mandate to NATO and, as per the statement of US interests in the Pentagon report above, extending global economic integration along market-friendly lines, these actions start to make sense (Graubart, 2013). Indeed, John Norris (2005, xxiii), a prominent state department official at the time, suggested that 'it was Yugoslavia's resistance to the broader trends of political and economic reform – not the plight of Kosovar Albanians – that best explains NATO's wars'. Recall also the first chapter on Libya. Stretching the UN mandate beyond protection to regime change, failing to support peace talks when there were genuine hopes of a breakthrough, and failing to even attempt to protect victims of opposition violence – including those in the ethnically cleansed town of Tawergha – all suggest that the character and interests of the interveners were major factors in the disaster in Libya. Indeed, they were a driving force behind the decision to pursue regime change even where steps towards it came at the expense of protecting people.

With this political context in mind we are now in a position to see what is wrong with the claim, introduced in Chapter 3, that those who helped create the crisis have additional duties to respond to it militarily. This claim is often based on an analogy in which a child is drowning. Fabre (2012, 190), for example, recognises that France had delivered weapons that were used to carry out the Rwandan genocide, only to conclude that 'in such cases it might stand to reason that France had a primary responsibility to intervene in the genocide as early as April 1994 – just as it behoves me, out of all available rescuers, to help the child I negligently pushed into the water'. Recall also her use of an analogy in which a murderer is not forbidden from saving a drowning child simply on account that they are a murderer. 'What matters, rather, is that he should be able to swim and rescue the child effectively – and then hand her over to appropriate parties' (Fabre, 2012, 189). This analogy distorts reality. Having detailed the extent and nature of already existing intervention, we can see that it is not the case that interveners have *negligently* pushed someone into a pond, or that they stumbled upon a child drowning (nor can they rescue them without causing "collateral damage"). Rather, would-be interveners are systematically engaging in interventions that stoke conflict. They also have agendas – including military projection and opening markets – that ensure that they carry out interventions in ways that kill, maim and provide cover for atrocity.[5] These agendas are aided and abetted by, and are not separate from, their military interventions. Indeed, the very military might that renders such actors able to engage in intervention – in the limited sense of having the material capacity to do so – stems precisely from their military projection, the resources they gain through uneven forms of trade and their destruction of the environment.

An interconnected world rife with already existing intervention is much more complex than the pond analogy suggests; there is a deep connection between a large number of murderers (and accomplices) and an even larger number of children who are constantly drowning – indeed being drowned – in various ponds. We could of course try to modify the pond scenario to accommodate these complexities and make it less distorting. Or develop a new example, perhaps one that starts with serial and unreformed arsonists being employed to build incinerators on the basis of their ability to set things on fire and being given rights to engage in otherwise restricted activities and use otherwise restricted materials in order to do so. But developing such examples would be pointless; the real world is a much better laboratory than the philosopher's pond could ever hope to be.

Once we abandon abstract and distorting thought experiments and instead look at actual cases, we see that the moral character of states has a decisive influence on how interventions play out. Inhumanitarian actions in Kosovo and Libya are not just based on miscalculations that will be corrected as relevant parties learn from experience. Rather, they are to be expected. And if concerned onlookers call for intervention, they should do so in full knowledge of the consequences that are likely to follow from intervention by bad international citizens with stated interests in spreading military bases, arms sales and favourable terms of trade. To join the choir calling for such actors to engage in protective military intervention serves only to give a veneer of legitimacy to their inhumanitarian, unprotective actions.

Legitimising moralistic militarism

So much, then, for the argument that bad international citizens can protect people responsibly by engaging in military interventions. But there is another reason as to why supporters of military humanitarianism and the R2P think that the interests of states can be reconciled with the aim of protection. Recall Dunne and Gelber (2015, 227), who admit that the 'motivations states have for supporting R2P may be driven by interests that have little or nothing to do with responsible sovereignty'. They go on to postulate, however, that this support can lead to 'large-scale historical change'. Beyond getting (or indeed not getting) humanitarian results in the short term through particular interventions, support for intervention also further develops the R2P norm. Such norm development will, in turn, improve responses to mass atrocities over time.

This hope that 'bad actors' can help develop 'good norms' is reflective of the way in which defenders of military intervention and architects of the R2P attempt to marry moralism with political realism (Dunne and Gelber, 2015, 227). On the one hand, they embrace – whether or not explicitly – the realist assumption that we cannot expect purported saviours to stop being as self-interested and harmful as they are. On the other, they assume that self-interest can be reconciled with the moral aim of protection through gradual norm-based change. The story of what enables this change should be familiar from Chapter 2. States' interests depend on their underlying identity. If states see themselves as agents that, amongst other things, protect civilians and save strangers – then their interest will be in protecting civilians and saving strangers. Norm-based change can thus lead to a reconciliation of self-interest and moral commitment that runs much deeper than the patchy and inconsistent – but nonetheless welcome – forms of "protection" that we are already beginning to see. The warriors for humanity are slowly beginning to crawl out of their realist cage. And the more they intervene, the more of a sign we have that their identity is changing such that they will do the morally right thing more consistently in future.[6] In fact, this is the only way to achieve moral progress in the long run: by working responsibly within 'the realm of the imminently possible' (Bellamy, 2015a, 103). To call for unrealistic political changes would only throw a spanner in the wheel of world-historical moral progress.

We have already seen that this story can be told (and believed) only when reality is deleted from the picture. As Chapter 2 pointed out, the institutionalisation of the R2P has taken place alongside an increase in atrocity crimes. But that is not the only problem. For this story also assumes that the R2P is an inherently progressive and civilising norm and that its further development can therefore only be a good thing. In making this assumption, the architects and defenders of the R2P find themselves very much in line with contemporary just war thinkers, who insist that the just war tradition is 'a tradition of generally condemning war' (May, 2008, 9) and has a 'disposition towards peace' (Evans, 2005, 15). Indeed, 'the aim of just war thinking is not justification (and certainly not glorification) of war, but containment' (Coates, 2016, 22, emphasis removed). The assumption in just war thinking and the R2P is that 'winding back the rules winds back restraints on organized violence and makes elimination a yet more remote ambition' (Bellamy, 2015a, 109).

This assumption is false. Norms and law concerning war and intervention do not work only as restraints. They can legitimise and sanitise violence, transforming it into violence that is perceived as good, "civilised", laudable and virtuous (Neu, 2017). Law and norms have become 'a political and ethical vocabulary for marking legitimate power and justifiable death' (Kennedy, 2006, 4). Think of the way in which drone strikes including signature strikes launched at (unknown) targets identified through algorithms are legitimised through legal and normative discourses (Espinoza and Afxentiou, 2018). Think also of torture sites like Guantánamo Bay which, though mistakenly seen as "black holes" or spaces of "exception" where law is absent, are in fact spaces in which 'a series of legal techniques operate' (Khalili, 2012, 66). Relatedly, far from conducting torture in spite of laws that prohibit it, US government-associated lawyers have *used* law in order to justify torture. In a now infamous 'torture memo', US lawyers including Jay Bybee (2002) wrote that 'physical pain amounting to torture must be equivalent in intensity to the pain accompanying serious physical injury, such as organ failure, impairment of bodily function, or death'; a definition which legitimises as lawful practices such as waterboarding and sensory deprivation. Much as law and norms can act as a restraint, they are also 'routinely mobilized as a strategic asset in war' (Kennedy, 2006, 11). They can 'provide an instrument of legitimation – albeit imperfect, incomplete, and fiercely contested' (Khalili, 2012, 67).

How does this pan out in terms of just war and the R2P? We agree that ideas matter and shape the context in which political decisions are made.[7] As we saw in Chapter 2, however, the R2P is not improving attempts to prevent and respond to mass atrocities. Instead, like the very idea of a just war, it legitimises a moralistic form of militarism.[8] By militarism, here, we refer to 'a set of attitudes and social practices which regards war and the preparation for war as normal and desirable social activity' (Mann, 1987, 35; see also Stavrianakis and Selby, 2012). And a *moralistic* militarism is one in which 'war and its attendant industries must be squared with normative commitments', principally, spreading humanitarian protection globally (Basham, 2018, 33).

There is an obvious sense in which the R2P – by putting pillar three military intervention on the table – broadens the repertoire of available justifications for war in international politics (if not in the tradition of just war). It does so by making it possible to justify wars as efforts to "save strangers", rather than as matters of self-defence and/or as attempts to avert threats to international peace and security (O'Connell, 2010). But beyond this, what does it mean to live in a world in which war is framed and perceived in this way? And what's so dangerous about this world?

Just war thinking and the R2P separate out "zones of civility" from "zones of barbarism", while also calling on actors in the "zones of civility" to fulfil their moral mission by waging just wars in order to save innocent victims of barbarism that takes place elsewhere. Occluded in this framework is the enduring violence of already existing intervention. Also occluded is the fact that states that often take up the humanitarian mantle – the UK and the USA – have fought more wars than anyone else in recent decades and are responsible for a huge amount of global military spending (Stavrianakis and Selby, 2012). With all of this erased from the picture, it becomes possible to assess acts of violence – intervention in Kosovo and Libya for instance – on a case-by-case basis without looking at the moral character of parties that are intervening; a moral character that is revealed in their wars in Afghanistan and Iraq, their contribution to everyday atrocity and their attempts to stoke conflict elsewhere. It then becomes possible for interveners to be presented as virtuous and agonised heroes willing to risk their lives in war in order to protect distant strangers from falling victim to atrocity crimes. The R2P norm thus works to normalise a perception according to which "doing good", pursuing interests, maintaining large military budgets and going to war can – and must – be reconciled. Only then can it be possible to think that the R2P is working in spite of – or perhaps even because of – global increases in arms trading.

There is an underlying belief here that virtue and militarism can be made to work together to produce a better world; that the problem of mass atrocity can be fixed, or at least ameliorated, without raising questions about the bad citizenship of would-be saviours. This is a dangerous illusion, and a moral climate in which it becomes normalised is not one in which the complex and multifaceted problem of mass atrocity can be understood, let alone addressed. Not only does this illusion distract from the vast array of changes to already existing intervention that are required to prevent atrocity. It also implies that there is *always* a need to be ready to go to war in order to save lives. For, as Gareth Evans (2009, 128), co-chair of the commission that coined the R2P, puts it, 'if there is one thing as bad as using military force when we should not, it is *not* using military force when we *should*'. Ability to use military force 'when we should' requires a permanent war machinery. Whilst such a machinery is already in place, the notion that it can fulfil humanitarian ends serves to justify, not challenge, its existence. This notion justifies the continued, perhaps even extended, presence of large stocks of weapons and trained armies, with all the expense and attendant infrastructure that comes with them. A humanitarian war machine also requires a wider culture in which life-saving wars are embraced as an integral feature of the public ethico-political imaginary; a culture that is sustained through everyday practices that celebrate and laud war. It demands, as a normalised and taken-for-granted part of wider public attitudes, a belief in the virtue of large-scale violence. And if we can learn one thing from the defence of the R2P, it is that these normalised attitudes can fundamentally shape our identity.

By understanding protection in this manner, just war thinking and the R2P fail to recognise that 'seemingly progressive' initiatives can contain 'the seeds' of their 'own complicity in broader systems of preparation for war and violence' (Stavrianakis, 2016, 844).[9] Those aiming to limit war and ensure that the rights of people are protected should turn in a different direction. As feminist scholars and activists have been saying for some time, limiting war and protecting people from mass atrocities requires leaving behind 'militarist logics that value hierarchical orders and the promotion of limited violence to ensure peace' (Wibben, 2018, 140; see also Enloe, 2007). Attempts to tackle atrocity must challenge, not reinforce, a militaristic moral climate.

◆ ◆ ◆

When we reject distorting frameworks that fail to address the real-world effects of humanitarian war and erase from view already existing intervention, it becomes clear that the R2P is a danger-ous norm. Not only does it fail, as we argued in Chapter 2, to improve attempts to prevent and respond to mass atrocity crimes. It also inspires calls to give additional powers of military interven-tion to actors who are already engaged in damaging political and economic interventions. In so doing it risks facilitating more dev-astating interventions like the one in Libya. More broadly, instead of focusing on the changes that are needed to prevent genocide, ethnic cleansing, war crimes and crimes against humanity, it cre-ates a moral climate in which military action by those already stoking crises is celebrated as a virtuous response that can help end mass atrocity for good. As such, even if we "extended" the remit of R2P to focus also on deeper forms of prevention, these efforts would remain tied to the militarism inherent in the R2P, potentially resulting only in a further militarisation of land govern-ance, environmental governance and development more broadly. In sustaining this militarist moral climate, the R2P's effect will not be to end mass atrocities once and for all. It will be to sustain amnesia about everyday atrocity, to disregard deeper forms of pre-vention and to legitimise military intervention performed by bad international citizens. The R2P is not the most we can hope for, nor should we attempt to work with it and add a deeper focus on prevention. We should step aside from the R2P and focus instead on non-violent means of protecting civilians. And we should call for changes to already existing practices of intervention that continue to create a world of mass atrocity.

Increasing the 'overall global pool of protection' in a world of everyday atrocity

If you are unwilling to join us in departing from just war thinking and the R2P, this section is for you.

Remember that any decision to intervene militarily to save the lives of others necessitates an evaluation of the consequences of intervention. We know that other-defending wars kill innocent civilians, destroy infrastructure, generate displacement, involve sexual violence and torture, and provide a cover for mass human rights violations. How can this be justified? Proportionality is a central part of any such justification. According to this principle, the morally good effects of the war must outweigh – or at least not be outweighed by – the negative effects of war (see, e.g., Coates, 2016, 209–234). The ICISS report that coined R2P explicitly invoked just war principles including proportionality and reasonable prospect of success. For a pillar three intervention to be justified there must 'be a reasonable chance of success in halting or averting the suffering which has justified the intervention, with the consequences of action not likely to be worse than the consequences of inaction' (ICISS, 2001, xii). This means that the existence of a just cause for intervention does *not* justify intervention when it will not have a net humanitarian benefit (or at least not when it is likely to make the situation worse). Bellamy takes this argument further, writing that 'in the world as we know it today it is not possible to protect everyone from genocide and mass atrocities all the time' (Bellamy, 2015a, 138). There are many cases that need to be addressed and the resources that can be committed to protection are finite. 'The harsh reality is that not everybody can be protected' (Bellamy, 2015a, 138). 'Sometimes', Bellamy continues, 'protection may be too expensive – the costs of protecting a particular population might be so high as to preclude the protection of others' (Bellamy, 2015a, 138). Thus, even where there is a just cause and a good probability of success, you may still need to decide between several possible cases of intervention and analyse which one will do more to increase humanitarian protection overall. This may mean that international action is inconsistent: some people get protected whilst others do not. But 'by protecting some people from genocide and mass atrocities, the overall global pool of protection increases' (Bellamy, 2015a, 138).

We do not share Bellamy's view that protecting everyone may be too expensive in financial terms – the military budgets of many states give some indication as to the extent of the resources that could be put towards protecting people or indeed towards ceasing to harm them such that they are better able to protect themselves. Nor do we share an approach that weighs human lives against each other and engages in quasi-mathematical calculations about how to protect the most people. But if it is the case that not all people can be protected, then there are important decisions to be made not only in relation to the various mass atrocity crimes that may be happening at a given time but also between acting to end atrocity crimes militarily and acting to stop, say, the extreme hunger experienced by 795 million of the world's people. Other-defending war is extremely expensive. Protective killing costs taxpayers a lot of money, not to mention the cost to lives and livelihoods it entails. And protecting through war reflects a choice in a world of limited resources; a choice that prevents resources and effort being directed towards the aim of protection through other, non-military means. To use the crude measure that just

(continued)

(continued)

war proportionality calculi tend to boil down to: we could use resources that go into "saving" some strangers by way of waging war in order to "save" other strangers from a different set of wrongs using protective means of a different sort. The failure to respond adequately to the Rwandan genocide in 1994, where 800,000 people died in 100 days of killing, is frequently invoked by proponents of military interventions (Müller and Wolff, 2014). But, as we saw in the previous chapter, it takes only 40 days for as many children under five to die primarily from easily avoidable causes. It takes less than 100 days for as many people to die – extremely painfully – from hunger alone. We know that something could be done about this, and that it would be relatively cheap – especially when compared with the military budgets of powerful states – to "save" thousands, perhaps tens of thousands, of lives every day (see, e.g., WHO, 2017a).

Instead of proposing to use available resources in a way that will dramatically 'increase the overall global pool of protection', advocates of humanitarian military interventions call for protective action that kills and maims innocents. This action is also extremely expensive, meaning that, in Bellamy's own logic, 'the costs of protecting a particular population might be so high as to preclude the protection of others' (Bellamy, 2015a, 138). If the aim is to increase the 'overall global pool of protection', then the R2P is not fit for purpose. And even if there might be some circumstances in which atrocity is so grave that for once military intervention would appear to be the most "cost-effective" way of increasing the pool of protection, this circumstance does not, as we shall now go on to reiterate in our concluding remarks on Rwanda, give reason to institutionalise a principle of military protection.

CONCLUDING REMARKS: GENOCIDE IN RWANDA AND CIVIL WAR IN SYRIA

Rwanda

Over the course of 100 days in 1994 around 800,000 people – mainly but not only Tutsis – were slaughtered in Rwanda. General Dallaire, head of the UN peacekeeping mission in Rwanda, had gained information about militia's training to kill Tutsis. His call for reinforcements and authorisation to destroy weapon caches was denied. Images of genocide beamed on televisions around the world. Dallaire claimed that just 5,000 extra troops would have been able to stop the genocide, in the short-term at least. But nothing was done to stop the killing.

Anyone who takes a position against intervention is inevitably going to be asked: "what about genocide in Rwanda?" This may seem like a strange question: Dallaire requested reinforcements for a peacekeeping force that was already there, not full-scale military intervention. Nonetheless, the case of Rwanda is taken to show that there can be (and indeed were) circumstances in which military intervention is justified. If our analysis is correct, the lesson that has usually been learnt from Rwanda – that we need to institutionalise a new principle of military protection – is the wrong one.

The Rwandan genocide was *not* a case of non-intervention. Genocide took place in the context of an array of devastating interventions. Chapter 4 returned frequently to Rwanda. Belgian colonial rule had racialised and fixed into place the very Hutu–Tutsi divide that was at the heart of genocidal violence. Rwanda was subject to a Structural Adjustment Programme that magnified tensions between Hutus and Tutsis and contributed – alongside other factors including the crash of coffee prices after the breakdown of the International Coffee Agreement – to severe economic problems. France provided Rwanda with vast stockpiles of weapons and trained some of the troops and militias who carried out the genocide (CLM, 2017). Following the publication of a report commissioned by the Rwandan government and compiled by a Washington law firm, Rwandan Foreign Minister Louise Mushikiwabo (cited in Moore, 2017) went as far as to claim that 'France was part of the planning, part of the conception, and part of the execution of the genocide'. Finally, genocide occurred in the immediate context of an internationally sponsored conflict resolution process and peacekeeping operation which 'not only failed to avert genocide, but even helped to create the conditions that made it possible' (Clapham, 1998, 193). Far from "standing aside", the international community was heavily involved in Rwanda and then withdrew, pulling out troops and other workers as the genocide started, and refusing to take with them Tutsis who were likely to be killed.

There are indeed lessons to be learnt from Rwanda, and one of them is that these already existing practices of intervention need to change radically. It is only through such change that something can be done about the everyday atrocity that sees tens of thousands of people die every day. And only then will it be possible to create a world in which genocide, ethnic cleansing, war crimes and crimes against humanity are less likely to occur. But as we showed in Chapters 3 and 4, contemporary just war thinking and the R2P simply delete these practices from the picture. As such, they fail to draw attention to the very things that need to be done in order to address the causes of atrocity – both everyday atrocity and directly physically violent atrocities like genocide in Rwanda. It is no surprise, therefore, that our analysis of the R2P's effectiveness in improving attempts to prevent and respond to mass atrocity, both in Libya and in terms of the wider record, was so damning. But it is all the more surprising to see that advocates are so fixated on protecting rights and minimising violence through means of war. Why do they advocate policies that are known to cause a lot of harm to a great many people, with positive outcomes being so radically uncertain? Why are they so concerned with preventing direct physical violence using military means, rather than with preventing *any* violence – whether direct or structural – through peaceful means?

This is a vital lesson. But it doesn't address directly that moment in Rwanda when people were being slaughtered; the moment when there was confidence that, at least for the time being (for the longer-term prognosis remained unclear), the slaughter could have been stopped at the cost of killing and maiming some people, but far fewer. So how to respond to such a situation as and when it happens? What are we to do, in other words, when it is already too late for longer-term prevention, when the dilemma is acute, when hundreds of thousands of people are being slaughtered over a matter of weeks?

This question is framed in a way that can work to silence critical voices. As Müller and Wolff (2014, 287) have argued, when the Rwandan genocide is separated from its context and used as *the* case that shows that military intervention is justified in general and that a framework like the R2P is required, it 'takes on a suspicious meaning'. 'It might be a tool to silence justified criticism and eliminate doubts on the wisdom of a proposed intervention by ascribing to opponents a willingness to condone large-scale homicide'. When physical slaughter is ongoing or imminent, it becomes a scandal to talk about other atrocities: about starvation, preventable diseases, environmental devastation and people drowning in the Mediterranean Sea. It is not that these atrocities stop happening at the dramatic moment at which the consciousness of humankind gets shocked. They are eliminated from view (if they had been seen in the first place). Likewise, it is seen to be outrageous, when people are currently being (or are about to be) massacred, to insist on an analysis of the various interventions that are already taking place and creating conditions in which genocides find their ideal habitat. Only a heartless monster could dare call for such analysis when what's at stake is the immediate survival of lots of people. It is almost as if the crisis itself works to silence analysis directed at understanding why it has come about in the first place, and how similar crises might be prevented in the future (Charlesworth, 2002). But if it is the case that these crises are not singular events in space and time, that they are instead located within a conflict-inducing context and will happen time and again for as long as this context persists: is it then not also the case that people who are genuinely concerned with stopping and preventing harm – and increasing 'the overall global pool of protection' – ought not to allow themselves to be drawn into paying exclusive attention to the immediate situation (Bellamy, 2015a, 138)?

Critics thus have very good responses to the "heartless monster charge". For example, they can ask: "why is it that you do not argue for putting an end to mass starvation, death through drowning and killing through environmental destruction, all of which are happening as we speak, with the same passion and dedication as you argue for the protection of people's rights through war?" Or, more drastically: "thousands of people are dying of malnutrition today, partly as a result of policies that you consistently fail to object to or fail to challenge with the same amount of energy. What's less urgent, immediate or conscience-shocking about that?"

What we are suggesting here is that one should refuse to be pulled onto the only terrain in which the adherents of violence tend to flourish: the terrain of extreme reductionism in which all that matters is the celebrated violent response to the immediate situation; a response directed at what are assumed to be disconnected villains who have allegedly turned up out of the blue. So whenever the critics are asked by supporters of military intervention, "but what are you going to do about this genocide *now?*", they need the courage to reply with a question of their own: "what are you going to do about mass starvation and mass drowning now? What are you going to do about arms sales and attempts to stoke tension? What are you going to do to make sure that we are not going to have this same conversation over and over again?" And when they are then charged with not respond-ing to the question that they have been asked, they should point out that the defenders of violence have consistently failed to respond to questions that *they* have been asked: "your consistent failure is precisely why we are even having this debate now – and why we will be having many more in the future". After all, a year before genocide in Rwanda, David Waller (1993, 60) wrote that 'Rwanda is on the brink of an uncharted abyss of anarchy and violence, and there are all too many historical, ethnic, eco-nomic, and political pressures that are likely to push it over the edge'. Warnings like Waller's will not be noticed, let alone acted upon, if we continue to work within a framework that thinks about mass atrocity crimes only as they are emerging, and that therefore fails to recognise political and economic pressures that produce them.

It remains true, however, that this conversation will not make the dilemma against which it is set go away. It is morally unbearable to live in the knowledge that other people are cur-rently being slaughtered – just as it is unbearable to live in the knowledge that other people are starving to death, drowning in the Mediterranean Sea and dying as a result of environmental destruction. Sometimes it is the case that situations arise where whatever one can do is wrong; where "you are damned if you do, and damned if you don't". Such is the situation of Sophie in the novel *Sophie's Choice*, where she is given the "choice", by the Nazis, to send one of her children to the gas chambers or see them both go. It is a serious mistake to think that we can articu-late moral blueprints that enable us to deal with these sorts of cases in a way which is "right". The very assumption that there is always a right answer, that morality never ceases to lose its ability to give action-guiding advice – even when such advice suggests that states ought to kill and maim innocents in order to prevent the killing and maiming of yet more innocents – may be one of the most vexing and harmful illusions of our times. A moral argument that knows no limits to the moral horrors it is prepared to justify is a bottomless pit. Such is the argument for just wars. It justifies far too much to be able to justify anything at all. There isn't always a right answer, and we should not pretend otherwise (Neu, 2017).

If we were to pretend otherwise, there would be no limits to what could potentially be called "right". It might then be right to slaughter a million innocents in order to save a billion. Or it might be right to torture a child for one hour to prevent the same child from being tortured for a whole day. And so on. When presented with these dilemmatic "choices", moral agency has been reduced or indeed eliminated; one can no longer "choose" on grounds of moral deliberation but only "pick" in a situation of utmost despair. In the face of these "choices" – which always hide from view all the other things that can and should be done to support people whose rights are being violated – the language of right vs. wrong loses its grip. Failure to recognise this effectively militates against the demand to prevent such dilemmas from arising in the first place. It fools us into thinking that we can remain virtuous while doing horrendous things. Morally speaking, all that can be said is that we have the duty to prevent these situations from occurring, that our current failure to meet this duty is colossal, and that the R2P has not even started to scratch the surface of this colossal failure.

The Rwandan genocide is not just presented as the paradigmatic case in which military intervention should have happened. Memory of it is also used to justify the institutionalisation of new norms and frameworks. Rwanda amounted to 'the abject failure of international society to honour humanity's promise to the Jews of "never again"', wrote Nicholas Wheeler (2000, 208) as part of a defence of a new norm of humanitarian intervention. And Rwanda was a shadow lingering over the International Commission on Intervention and State Sovereignty (ICISS) report which gave rise to the R2P. It was so abhorrent that we simply *must* institutionalise new principles to respond to it. But this move should not be made so quickly. Even if you, the reader, would come down on the side of full-scale military intervention in Rwanda, this does not mean that you should support the institutionalisation of other-defending war and the R2P. When a move is made from focusing on the particular case of Rwanda to the more general case for intervention and the institutionalisation of new norms and potentially new laws, it is crucial to account for what happens when the moralism of the R2P hits the ground of real-world politics. In the world as we know it, the R2P can never be the sort of thing that has been dreamt up in its advocates' minds. Rather, as we argued in Chapter 5, it legitimises a moralistic militarism and an attendant war machinery. It gives wars conducted by bad international citizens a veneer of legitimacy and frames them as "civilised" and virtuous.

This is the paradox of military humanism. Supporters of the R2P don't take their commitment to political realism far enough. They think that what they defend can become a genuine moral tool in the hands of selfish states within the regimes of power that presently characterise global politics. At the same time, their political realism goes too far in excluding the possibility of deeper change. In so doing, they acquiesce in the notion that the best we can hope for is a happy reconciliation of moral virtue and hard-nosed self-interest – a reconciliation which, as we have demonstrated, is not possible. The R2P does not represent any moral progress. It is a step in the wrong direction, for it does not offer any prospect for the deeper transformations that can – perhaps – end mass atrocity once and for all.

Even if you, our imagined reader, think that full-scale military intervention would have been preferable in Rwanda, this is no reason for you to support the further development of the R2P or indeed to think that the problem of mass atrocity can be solved by waging purportedly just wars. Let us not be drawn into the moralistic militarism of the R2P. Let us call instead for wider and deeper changes – ignored in the R2P – to ensure that we can say "never again" and mean it.

Syria

As we write the final parts of this book, eastern Ghouta is under siege. Civilians are dying under bombs and potentially under chemical weapons. A ceasefire, agreed only after attempts by Russia to delay a Security Council decision, is being violated. As always, simplistic media narratives belie the complexity of the situation and tell particular stories for particular purposes. Some focus exclusively on the vicious way in which the Assad regime and its Russian supporters are killing innocents. This narrative is furthered by the rapid circulation of images – some from Ghouta but some, which were shared over 125,000 times on Twitter, that were later revealed to be from Gaza in Palestine and Mosul in Iraq. Other media narratives focus exclusively on the way in which rebels are forcing civilians to stay in Ghouta so that they can be used as human shields. The comparisons with Aleppo are haunting. Meanwhile, in the Afrin canton in the north of Syria, Turkish planes – with permission to fly from Russia – are bombing Kurdish-Syrian People's Protection Units (YPG) and Syrian Democratic Forces who, in turn, are fighting with support and weapons from the USA. Syrian government militias (who, in other parts of Syria, are fighting with support from Russia and encountering opposition from groups supported and armed by the USA) have arrived to support Syrian Democratic Forces. The complexity is dizzying, with alliances varying across regions. And the effects are chilling – 'the shelling and bombing of houses, the mangled bodies of children killed by the explosions'. Despite the continuing death, destruction, displacement and mass human rights violations, events in Afrin 'are almost entirely ignored by both media and foreign politicians' (Cockburn, 2018).[1]

Faced with the question of what's to be done in Syria, there are no simple solutions. We have seen throughout this book that the case for humanitarian military intervention breaks down. It can be made only through analyses that exclude from the picture the devastating effects of past humanitarian wars, and the already existing practices of intervention that stoke conflict. We have also argued that it is dangerous to give additional powers of military intervention to actors already engaged in devastating economic and political interventions.

We can offer answers that are at once so easy to give and so difficult to implement. Humanitarian rescue missions are needed to get food in and civilians out. All sides should stop fuelling militarism and do all they can to get parties to and people affected by the conflict around a negotiating table. This will not provide an immediate fix. But that an answer is so difficult should not draw us towards the false idols of just war and the R2P. To intervene militarily would kill and maim innocent people, potentially make the situation worse and, in the context of the complex, internationalised conflict that is Syria, risk escalating into a world war pitting nuclear powers against one another. And yet all other options appear insufficient. Even if they won't immediately stop the conflict, various non-violent measures should be taken: refugees should be supported and not left to drown, turned away and/or vilified; all attempts should be made to broker talks and ceasefires; and ongoing attempts to stoke and benefit from tensions should be stopped immediately. Beyond that, a key commitment should be to do everything possible to avoid such situations occurring in the future. The R2P will not do this. It gives us false hope – false hope that we can intervene militarily, and false hope that, over time and in the absence of the much bigger and more demanding changes, a rhetorical commitment to protection will eventually put an end to mass atrocity crimes. Embracing such false hope obscures from view the work that is needed. What is needed is a more radical set of changes which will require 'sustained, popular struggle' (Graubart, 2013, 90).

Sustained popular struggle already exists and offers a source of real hope. Feminist peace movements from the Mothers Front in Sri Lanka (de Alwis, 2009) to the Women of Greenham Common in the UK (Eschle, 2017) have consistently challenged militarism, emphasising 'the need to work to prevent conflict through attention to social and economic inequalities both within and across states' (Heathcote, 2014, 126). In so doing, feminist peace activists offer 'a method and a means for speaking about peace through disarmament, through attention to the continuum of violence from the intimate to the international, and through identifying the persistence of gender-based violence in communities defined as peaceful and in those enduring conflict'. A large transnational peasant movement has demonstrated the damage done by land grabs, calling for peasants' rights and food sovereignty as a way to cool the planet, feed the world and undo the violence of land grabbing (Martínez-Torres and Rosset, 2010). Anti-militarist movements including Campaign Against the Arms Trade are working to challenge the arms trade in particular and militarism more broadly through a range of means including legal advocacy, direct action and awareness raising (Wearing, 2016; May, 2015; Rossdale, forthcoming). This is before we begin to look at the range of grassroots environmental movements across the world that call for meaningful attempts to address environmental destruction and enact alternatives to development that put people, communities and nature first (Shiva, 2014). These activists are at the forefront of the battle against the structural forms of violence that reproduce a world in which the atrocity of mass avoidable death takes place as a matter of routine, and in which atrocities like those in Rwanda and Syria continue to emerge. It is here, and not with just war and the R2P, that we should place our energy. And it is only through this widening of their moral concern and analytical gaze that scholars and activists can challenge, and not be complicit with, the structural violence and militarism that serve only to reproduce a world of mass atrocity.

NOTES

Introduction

1 Unless otherwise stated, all references to conflict in this book relate specifically to *violent* conflict.

2 Recent introductions to the just war tradition include Bellamy (2006); Coates (2016); and Orend (2013). See Dower (2009) for a very useful introduction that is less entrenched in the tradition.

3 Brian Orend (2013, 42), for example, thinks that war may be waged only by 'a minimally just or legitimate state'.

4 These are the *jus ad bellum* criteria, which regulate the waging of war. Not all just war theorists would subscribe to exactly these six criteria, nor would all of them understand them in the same way. A related set of *jus in bello* criteria regulate war's conduct. More recently, theorists have also reflected on *jus post bellum* – justice in the ending and aftermath of war. See Fabre (2012, 4–5) for an introduction to these different areas of just war thinking.

5 For accounts that trace this dimension in the just war tradition, see Bass (2009); Chesterman (2001); and Simms and Trim (2011).

6 As Rengger (2013, 63) writes, 'the period since the end of the Second World War, and most especially the period from the 1970s to the present, has seen a revival of normative theorizing about war unparalleled since the seventeenth century'.

7 Walzer (2011), however, was against the intervention in Libya in 2011.

8 They would also, Fabre (2012, 170) continues, '[assign] the status of a just cause for intervention to a greater range of human rights violations than non-cosmopolitans would be willing to accept'.

9 As just war thinker Jeff McMahan (2004, 80) puts it, 'when humanitarian intervention is justified, there can be no right of national defense against it, least of all by the state that is the agent of the persecution that provides the just cause for the intervention'.

10 We say 'the principle (if not practice)' because sovereignty has been a myth for much of the concept's history, during which the world was made of empires and colonies, not sovereign states.

11 Between 1945 and 1991, only three military interventions which could be seen to be in part about the protection of people from mass atrocities took place: India's on behalf of Bengalis in the Bangladesh war of 1971; Vietnam's against

Pol Pot in Cambodia in 1978–1979; and Tanzania's in Uganda in 1978–1979. The 1990s, by contrast, saw a whole series of interventions – in Iraq, Somalia, Haiti, Bosnia and Kosovo – which were considered to have humanitarianism as at least part of their rationale. This new role for the international community is reflected in the fact that between 1990 and 1994 twice as many UN Security Council resolutions were passed as during the first 45 years of UN history (Weiss, 2004, 136).

12 In its initial formulation, the R2P also included a responsibility to rebuild after mass atrocities. The responsibility to rebuild has since played only a minor role in academic reflection on and policy advocacy for the R2P.

13 This first pillar builds on the idea of 'responsible sovereignty' developed by Francis Deng, a Sudanese diplomat, affiliate of the US-based Brookings Institution and former (1994–2004) Representative of the UN Secretary-General on internally displaced persons (Deng et al., 1996). He claimed that governments that do not fulfil their responsibilities to protect forfeit their sovereignty, and used this idea in his diplomacy to encourage political leaders to ensure that they protect their populations as a means of protecting their sovereignty. He (2010, 84) would say to leaders that 'you must be seen to be protecting your people or else you risk intervention', always placing emphasis on the importance of retaining sovereignty. In this respect, the R2P is, as Ban ki-Moon (UN, 2009, paragraph 6) said in his first report on it, 'an ally of sovereignty, not an adversary. It grows from a positive and affirmative notion of sovereignty as responsibility, rather than from the narrower idea of humanitarian intervention. By helping states to meet their core protection responsibilities, the R2P seeks to strengthen sovereignty, not weaken it'. But as Mamdani (2010) argues, this does not mean that the R2P is no threat to state sovereignty (see Chapter 3, note 6).

14 To give an example, whilst Bellamy has claimed as a great success of R2P the African Union mediation during post-electoral violence in Kenya in 2007–2008, the then African Union Chairperson Jean Ping (Pergantis, 2014, 311) 'publicly questioned the view that the African Union-led political mediation under the Kenyan conflict constituted an intervention under the R2P concept'. The repackaging of existing measures of, amongst other things, peacebuilding, preventative diplomacy and mediation as part of the R2P has been controversial. This is particularly so in relation to attempts to repackage civilian protection measures as part of the R2P. Key policy voices from the ICISS to the Special Advisor on the R2P have made great efforts to keep the R2P and wider norms of humanitarian protection separate. The reason for this is that a principle which has, even only in part, a military aspect will

inevitably generate controversy and put those against whom the principle is invoked on the defensive. The possibility of military intervention can generate, and in cases like Dafur has generated, major problems for humanitarian aid workers, who may be deemed "Trojan horses" opening the way to military intervention. This suspicion that they may be present for reasons that go beyond politically neutral humanitarian aid work can result in aid workers being denied access. Reflecting on years of humanitarian aid work and emergency relief co-ordination, John Holmes (2014, 145) has suggested that the possibility of military intervention can have a negative effect on aid work: 'too much loose chatter about intervention, when there was little chance of any such thing happening, was in practice unhelpful and damaging'. It was damaging politically on the basis that it led rebels and their supporters to think that, in light of the prospect for external support, they need not take negotiations seriously. It was also damaging from a humanitarian perspective, for aid workers were sometimes punished and denied access when the international community acted against the Sudanese President Omar Al-Bashir. Stephen Hopgood has gone as far as to suggest that the R2P stands in the way of attempts to prevent atrocities against civilians. The post-2001 emphasis on R2P, Hopgood (2014, 181) claims, 'actually reduced the chances of truly humanitarian action by complicating the calculations of sovereigns faced with unpredictable political risks'. For Hopgood (2014, 183), the R2P is therefore best understood as 'a decade-long interlude, a diversion from the underlying trend toward establishing a post-Cold War norm of preventing atrocities against civilians'.

15 These pillars are not sequential. 'There is no set sequence to be followed from one pillar to another, nor is it assumed that one is more important than another' (UN, 2009, 2). Were they to be sequenced, international assistance and capacity building (pillar two) would only ever arrive too late, when a state had already proven unwilling or unable to protect its population from the four crimes.

1 The catastrophic failure of intervention in Libya

1 This is not to say that no rape took place in the Libyan civil war, nor that it was not used as a weapon of war.

2 Kuperman (2013) argues that these figures – combined with the fact that the bodies were all male and adult – show that Qaddafi's regime was not targeting civilians. On the contrary, reports do suggest that the regime attacked civilians. But they did not do so on anything like the scale of Rwanda and Srebrenica. See, for instance, OHCHR (2012) and International Crisis Group (2011).

3 On 13 January 2012, Zuma (in Nesbitt, 2012) repeated his claim that the resolution was 'largely abused', this time speaking on behalf of the African Union.

4 This defence is often repeated in scholarship on the R2P (see, for instance, Bellamy, 2015a; Paris, 2014; and Vilmer, 2016). Vilmer (2016, 28) also defends NATO from claims that the use of ground forces in Libya constituted mission creep.

5 The Inquiry of the High Commissioner on Libya states that whilst Qaddafi did attack protestors, 'the commission has not found evidence that one particular group was targeted more than others' (OHCHR, 2012).

6 The UN Human Development Index gives countries an overall human development score based on life expectancy, education levels and per capita income.

7 Kuperman (2013) also claims that intervention in Libya may be one of the reasons for the worsening situation in Syria. Support for rebels in Libya may, Kuperman speculates, have encouraged rebels in Syria to step up their insurgency in the hope that they would then receive international support to overthrow Assad.

2 As the world burns, we bathe in the glory of a new norm of protection

1 In comparison to the ICISS report, the World Summit Outcome Document specifies a narrower remit for the R2P, saying that it relates only to the four crimes of genocide, ethnic cleansing, crimes against humanity and war crimes. The ICISS report referred, more broadly, to crimes that shock the conscience of humanity. It included as an example of such crimes situations in which states were unable or unwilling to respond adequately to natural disasters. Later, in 2008, the government of Burma refused to allow international humanitarian relief workers access to devastated regions after Cyclone Nargis. In response, then French Foreign Secretary Bernard Kouchner claimed that the international community had a responsibility to protect those in Burma and called for military intervention to provide safe access for humanitarian workers. His request was flatly rejected, with Security Council discussions making clear that the R2P applies only to the four crimes and not to natural disasters (Junk, 2016).

2 An earlier draft suggested that the international community had an *obligation* to use diplomatic, humanitarian and other peaceful means. US Ambassador John Bolton insisted that this language be watered down by replacing the term "obligation" with "responsibility" (see Loiselle, 2013). We are not arguing that this watering down of the R2P is a bad thing. On the

contrary, if our arguments in this book are correct, the R2P would be even more dangerous if it were not watered down.

3 For a different account see Orford (2011), who argues that, far from introducing a new set of ideas that may in turn inspire new practices, the R2P codifies a set of changes that had already happened in practice.

4 The same argument was also used a decade earlier. Wheeler (2000) claimed that condemnation of the failure to stop genocide in Rwanda showed that the expected standards of behaviour in international society had changed, with a failure to respond to genocide deemed unacceptable and a reason for censure. That the very same argument is still made in relation to atrocities that took place 15 years after the "expected standards" in international society had apparently changed might give reason to be cautious when celebrating the efficacy of norm-based change.

5 There are heated debates about whether the R2P did galvanise consensus behind intervention in Libya. Loiselle (2013) points out that R2P language referred only to the responsibility of the Libyan state, and not to the responsibility of the international community. Hehir (2013) argues that the decision to intervene in Libya was based on exceptional circumstances and reflected only the 'permanence of inconsistency' in Security Council practice. Hehir (2015, 222) is critical of norm-based abstraction more broadly, claiming that 'there is a need for analysis, comparative reflection and evidence that … references to R2P are more than just high-sounding tokenism'.

6 This focus on high-level discussions and the primary concern with the R2P's progress as a norm has continued post-Libya. After early celebrations of the success of the R2P in Libya, the NATO intervention came under fire. When responding to the backlash from Brazil, South Africa and others after NATO's perceived mission creep, R2P scholars are concerned first and foremost with what this backlash means for the future development of the R2P norm. Gareth Evans (2011), for instance, suggested that the R2P norm had taken two steps forward, one step back. The problems associated with Libya were 'the inevitable teething problems associated with the evolution of any major international norm' (Evans, 2012, 18). Others have seen the backlash to NATO's mission creep as a key factor in subsequent Security Council gridlock over the abuse of civilians in Syria. For Ramesh Thakur (2013, 61), 'the price of exceeding the mandate there [in Libya] has been paid by Syrians'. The cost of exceeding the mandate is not seen to be experienced by civilians in Libya. It is a cost that is felt, first of all, at the level of the development of the norm, and then by civilians in Syria who have felt the effects of backlash against the norm. Since the costs are felt at the level of the R2P norm, the

solution is deemed to lie in the refinement of the norm. Evans, for instance, places great hope in an addition to the principle, suggested to the UN by Brazil, of a commitment to 'responsibility while protecting'. Relatedly, Dunne and Gerber (2014, 330) argue that the controversies over Libya resulted from 'the contradictory statements offered in support of the action by those governments involved in implementing the mandate, and their abject failure to maintain consistency in relation to arguing around the R2P norm'. As before, the primary purpose of engaging in this diagnosis is to take further the norm. The importance of consistent argumentation in the Security Council, Dunne and Gelber (2014, 328) argue, 'needs to be better understood in order to facilitate the future traction of the R2P norm in international negotiations'. Even after Libya, then, the real-world effects of military intervention drop out of the picture, replaced with a story of the stuttering but persistent development of an international norm.

7 Failure to focus on the realities of intervention is not new. Reflecting on earlier humanitarian intervention debates, Adam Roberts (1999, 110) identified 'a consistent failure to address directly the question of the methods used in such interventions'. Kurt Mills and Cian O'Driscoll (2010) identified the same problem a decade later.

8 The two studies that do make this argument are Seybolt (2007) and Krain (2005). Of the other two studies, one concludes that it is not possible to solve a conflict by 'simply intervening per se'. Instead, co-ordination with other involved third parties is required (Balch-Lindsay and Enterline, 2000, 24). The other (Fortna, 2008, 6) focuses only on peacekeeping *after* a ceasefire has been reached and explicitly rules out of its remit preventative deployments of troops, attempts to broker and make peace, and military interventions to bring about an end to hostilities.

9 Bellamy (2015a, 40n5) claims that studies that show that intervention can have negative effects conflate all types of intervention. This is not the case in Peksen's study, which disaggregates data according to whether interventions are supportive, hostile or neutral with respect to the state. It also looks at the different effects of interventions led by states with different political regimes, finding that 'interventions led by liberal democracies are unlikely to be different from other interventions' (Peksen, 2012, 566).

10 Bellamy (2015a, 66) acknowledges the difference between the R2P working as a rallying call and 'the effectiveness of international policies themselves', stating that the two issues should not be conflated. The R2P 'may be effective as a rallying call and yet the policies pursued as a result might prove less than wholly effective'. Despite this acknowledgement, Bellamy uses this data

as a key part of his book-length defence of the R2P and uses similar, albeit slightly more detailed, data as a key part of an article in which he argues that the R2P 'has become an established international norm *associated with positive changes to the way that international society responds to genocide and mass atrocities*' (Bellamy, 2015b, 161, emphasis added). In making this claim on the basis of his evidence of R2P's effect as a rallying call, Bellamy fails to follow his own warning and conflates the R2P's effectiveness as a rallying call with its effectiveness in improving responses to mass atrocities.

11 Bellamy (2015a, 100) claims that the responsibility to protect helped secure a 'negotiated transition of authority in Yemen'. This stands in stark contrast to UN Secretary-General Ban ki-Moon's (UN, 2015a, 5) assessment of Yemen as one of several cases in which 'international efforts failed to deliver adequate protection'.

12 The Uppsala Conflict Data Program dataset is based on news reporting and records battle-related deaths caused by direct physical violence. We use this data not out of any conviction that it provides a comprehensive analysis of violent conflict over time but to criticise accounts of the success of the R2P on the terrain that defenders themselves occupy. Beyond this footnote we opt against pointing to the problems with using this data to make inferences concerning the overall record of the R2P. First of all, Uppsala data does not register the range of avoidable deaths that occur in war through the destruction of infrastructure, displacement and resultant poverty, the loss of food resources as people flee areas in which food is grown, and so on. Second, it records deaths only when it can identify a perpetrating actor (be it a government, a rebel group or an international party to the conflict). Taken together, these two features result in very low counts of deaths in war. Whilst Uppsala data records 20,494 battle-related deaths in Iraq between 2003 and 2006, a different study found that 655,000 Iraqis had died as a result of conflict in Iraq between March 2003 and July 2006 (Burnham et al., 2006). This study focused on all the deaths that result from war (and not just direct battle-related deaths). It calculated these overall deaths by asking a sample of the affected population whether they knew of people who had been killed. Third, the classification of conflicts in Uppsala data is controversial and tends to underplay the role played by international actors. To give an example, the governments of Australia, the UK and the USA are registered as being in conflict in Iraq only up until the establishment of the Coalition Provisional Authority one month after the initial invasion in 2003. All other killing becomes the responsibility of the Iraqi government and a variety of rebel groups, despite the ongoing involvement of coalition forces (see, for

instance, Khalili, 2012). Fourth and on a different note, there are fundamental limits to any understanding of war based on data and statistics, which tell us little about how conflicts are felt, framed and understood.

13 Michael Walzer does not use these sorts of fictional thought experiments. However, as we shall argue in the following chapter, he distorts his object of analysis by separating out "zones of civility" and "zones of barbarism".

14 Here, we take up Frowe's example of the USA. We might equally have suggested that each Russian war be given a fair chance of being morally justified, on a case-by-case basis and in abstraction from Russia's imperial history and expansionist ambition. Doing so would, however, be quite unfamiliar in contemporary just war thinking. For despite the pretence of universalism, the latter remains parochial: it tends to ask the question, for instance, of whether the US war against Iraq was just, and not the question of whether Iraq was justified in fighting back against the US (see Neu, 2017, 14).

15 Elsewhere, one of us has referred to this desire to separate issues as a form of 'analytic atomism', arguing that the separation of justifications of torture, war and sweatshop labour from a discussion of the wider context in which these practices occur plays a crucial role in justifying the violence associated with such practices (Neu, 2017).

3 Zones of civility and zones of barbarism: the internalist diagnosis of mass atrocity crimes

1 In making this claim, we move beyond a focus on war and intervention to offer an overarching critique of the way in which R2P is framed. Recall that the R2P, in its first and second pillars, is focused, respectively, on state responsibility and the prevention of mass atrocity crimes. While the first pillar locates the blame for mass atrocity crimes with the state in which they emerge (see Whyte, 2017), the second pillar fails to recognise the way in which the international community could help prevent mass atrocities by changing the ways in which it already intervenes.

2 United Nations (UN) Secretary-General Ban ki-Moon (UN, 2014, paragraph 79) describes the R2P as 'narrow but deep: narrow because it is restricted to the protection of populations from atrocity crimes [genocide, war crimes, ethnic cleansing and crimes against humanity], but deep given the array of measures required for its implementation'. For advocates, this narrow remit allows for focused attention on mass atrocities and for the design of precise measures to address the specificities of such egregious crimes. Were the principle broadened out, supporters argue, such a deep response would be impossible. States – despite having signed up to much broader principles

focusing on a much larger range of wrongs in the form of human rights dec-larations and conventions (see Karp, 2015) – would not accept such deep and potentially intrusive measures. Our argument here is that the narrow focus of the R2P hides from view the deep responses, which include changing already existing practices of intervention and addressing everyday atrocity, that would help prevent mass atrocity crimes.

3 For a related critique, see Brown and Bohm (2016).

4 Hilary Charlesworth (2010, 244) argues that, in all of its pillars, the R2P requires 'top-down intervention, with little emphasis on empowering local people, particularly women'. The Secretary-General's 2014 report, written after this critique, confirms that Charlesworth's words still ring true.

5 Orford (1999, 695) writes that 'in such intervention stories, the international community plays the role of the masculine, active hero, while states targeted for intervention occupy the position of the secondary, passive victim. The sub-ject of that narrative, the international community, is the character able to act in the world, to imagine, create and bring about new worlds. Agency is only held by the international community, international organizations, or the US'.

6 Mamdani (2010, 54) argues that the global regime of R2P bifurcates the international order between, on the one hand, sovereign states whose cit-izens have political rights, and, on the other, de facto trusteeship territories whose populations are seen as 'wards in need of external protection'. This is because the R2P renders sovereignty conditional upon responsible protec-tion only for 'those states defined as "failed" or "rogue"'. Whilst all states are formally responsible for protecting their population, in reality only weaker states will be subject to intervention. It is therefore only weaker states – often deemed "failed" or "rogue" – that have sovereignty as authority only on the condition that they fulfil their responsibility to protect. What results 'is a bifurcated system whereby state sovereignty obtains in large parts of the world but is suspended in more and more countries in Africa and the Middle East' (Mamdani, 2010, 54). This bifurcation also re-invokes framings associated with colonial rule. On the one hand, we have 'racialised, vulner-able others residing in the global South' who are 'in dire need of protection' (Pourmokhtari, 2013, 1774). On the other, we have those 'civilised Northern states' that 'exercise a self-assigned heroic and civilising duty', potentially by waging war to save those who need protection (Pourmokhtari, 2013, 1774; see also Ayoob, 2002). Gareth Evans (2009, 56) has suggested that the notion that R2P 'only applies to weak and friendless countries, never strong ones' is one of five major misunderstandings of the R2P: *all* states have a responsibility to protect, not just weaker ones. Whilst this may be true in

principle, in reality it is only states that are relatively weak and friendless who will be subject to any unwanted intervention that may be authorised through the R2P. Such authorisation will come only when stronger countries are willing to exercise pressure on weaker ones or when countries are isolated – as Libya was – with no friends willing to stand up for them in Security Council or other negotiations. Moreover, one of the criteria in justifying interventions against the will of the state is the probability of a good outcome. It is hard to see how a good humanitarian outcome could come from the international community waging war against China, Russia, India, Israel or the USA, given the military power of these countries.

7 Walzer's (2004, xi) bracketing of the indecency of the 'supposedly decent' divulges his musings on empire as mere lip-service to features of the material world that he chooses to exclude from what he has established as the relevant field of analysis. More broadly, just war thinking focuses our attention on the immediate issues at stake before the war begins. In the case of the 2003 Iraq war, for example, focus falls on inspections, disarmament, hidden weapons and so on – and then on the conduct of the war. Just war thinking thus avoids questions about the global struggle for resources and power. It is as if citizens of the ancient world had focused narrowly on the conflict between Rome and some other city-state over whether a treaty had been violated, as the Romans always claimed in the lead-up to their attack, without ever discussing the long history of Roman expansion.

8 Fabre (2012, 189) does note that 'a potential intervener who is unable or unwilling to carry out the intervention without infringing fundamental requirements such as non-combatant immunity cannot be regarded as a legitimate belligerent'. This arises in the context of a discussion of whether regimes that are not 'rights-respecting communities', such as dictatorships, can wage humanitarian wars. Her conclusion is that *in principle* they *can*, although *in practice* it may be the case that their interventions are illegitimate on account that they are unlikely to be effective in fulfilling humanitarian ends. Notice, first, that this is only a potential problem *in practice*. The real-world character of states does not have any bearing on the in-principle justification according to which war can be fought by '*whomever* is in a position to protect the victims' (Fabre, 2012, 188, emphasis added). Second, Fabre (2012, 189) seems to suggest that the character of states is an in-practice constraint for states, like dictatorships, that do not respect individual rights at home. In this regard, Fabre points out that 'a community which respects the rights of its own members is more likely, perhaps, to conduct the humanitarian war justly and to realize its just ends'. The

global injustices stemming from the actions of purportedly rights-respecting regimes – from patents, protectionism and plunder – drop out of the picture. As we shall argue in Chapter 5, this is a dangerous error, for the moral character of purportedly rights-respecting regimes has a decisive impact on how their interventions are carried out, rendering them inhumanitarian and unprotective.

9 Relatedly, Fabre (2012, 181) suggests that 'if there are a number of victim communities, and if a potential rescuing regime is not in a position to help them all but is in part responsible for the predicament of one of them, the fact of its responsibility for those wrongdoings may well justify holding it under a duty to help that particular community rather than others'.

10 Indeed, Laurie Calhoun (2013, 81), writes that 'the continual depletion and replenishment of stockpiled weapons is necessary for the capitalized weapons industry to perpetuate itself, and it would be naïve to suppose that corporate leaders and the politicians whom they support are somehow immune from these economic forces'.

4 Everyday atrocity and already existing intervention

1 Galtung (1990, 292) 'see[s] violence as avoidable insults to basic human needs, and more generally to *life*, lowering the real level of needs satisfaction below what is potentially possible'. Rather than engage in extensive theoretical discussion of structural violence, we opt to show how it manifests itself in practice.

2 These are by no means the only forms of already existing intervention that contribute to the emergence of mass atrocity. For instance, much has already been written on links between extractive industries and conflict (Bannon and Collier, 2003). Resource extraction, too, is a complex, collaborative exercise involving states in the global North and the global South (Comaroff and Comaroff, 2012) and an exercise that exploits inadequacies in international legal frameworks (Wenar, 2016).

3 These are World Health Organization estimates. The Uppsala Conflict Data Program estimate is 119,000 for the same year.

4 Focusing on nutrition would result in an even starker picture, given that numerous people consume sufficient calories without getting the nutrients that they need (see, e.g., Bellows et al., 2016).

5 Available estimates vary. Some suggest that a death from hunger takes place every second. Others, informed by a *Lancet* study, suggest that a child dies a hunger-related death every 10 seconds. The UN World Food Programme has a lower estimate of child hunger-related mortality, suggesting that

45 per cent of child deaths per year are hunger-related, which works out at one child dying for hunger-related reasons every 20 seconds. Here, we have taken a relatively conservative estimate for the number of people (children and adults) who die from hunger each year. Our figure is taken from Hunger and World Poverty (2017), which draws on data from the UN World Food Program, Oxfam and Unicef.

6 We have space here only to offer fragments of this global history and enduring present. For more, see, e.g., Davis (2002); Escobar (1995); Galeano (2009); Lugones (2010); Mignolo (2011); and Shiva (2014).

7 Bellamy (2015a, 103–105), for instance, has responded to criticisms of the absence of gender in the R2P by suggesting that these are addressed elsewhere as part of the UN Women, Peace and Security agenda.

8 For this reason, Abouharb and Cingranelli (2006, 234) call for 'existing theories of repression' to be 'revised to take greater account of transnational causal factors'. See also Hippler (1995, 24), who notes that structural adjustment reforms involve huge cuts to government social and economic programmes, leaving the state only with 'the police, the army and the secret service: the instruments of repression'.

9 Despite global moves in the direction of "sustainable development" and the signing of the Paris Agreement on Climate Change in 2016, action on climate change remains inadequate. Here is not the place to recount the various green critiques of these initiatives, but as a start one might note that the pledges in the Paris Agreement are non-binding and unlikely to be sufficient to keep us to the agreed target of a maximum global temperature increase of 1.5 degrees Celsius. Moreover, they do not kick in until 2020. At the current rate of emissions, the maximum amount of carbon that can be emitted to keep temperature increases to 1.5 degrees Celsius would be all but emitted by the time the Paris Agreement enters into effect (Hickel, 2017).

10 Literature under the "environmental security" or "eco-scarcity" label has looked at the relationship between violent conflict on the one hand and a variety of scarcities linked to environmental change – water, land and so on – on the other. The expectation is that environmental changes will lead to resource scarcity, which will intensify inter-group fighting over resources. Alternatively, environmentally induced migration may lead to new competition over resources, which will in turn magnify fault lines between ethnic or class groups and thereby increase the likelihood of violent conflict. Findings have been mixed. Studies have indicated strong links between environmentally induced scarcities and conflict in Rwanda (Baechler, 1999; Ohlsson, 2000), Kenya (Kahl, 2006), South Africa (Homer-Dixon and Blitt, 1998), Sudan

(Suliman, 1997), Burundi (Bundervoet, 2009), Syria (Gleick, 2014) and else-where. These findings have been contested, however. Theisen (2008) found that the study identifying the strongest links between environmental factors and violent conflict (Hauge and Ellingsen, 1998) could not be replicated. More broadly, numerous studies have 'found, at best, modest support for eco-scarcity thinking' (Theisen, 2008, 802). Mixed findings should come as no sur-prise. Notwithstanding the various methodological issues with environmental security literature (see, e.g., Ide, 2017; van Leeuwen and van der Haar, 2016), violent conflicts result from the complex interaction of multiple factors and not from the presence of resource scarcity alone. Jon Barnett (2000, 287) has written a scathing critique of environmental security literature, diagnosing its failure to recognise that the major forms of existing environmental insecurity are precisely the insecurities felt by people who suffer from displacement, dis-ease and so on. In ignoring these and focusing instead on the violent conflict that may or may not stem from environmental change, environmental secu-rity literature also 'obscures Northern complicity in the generation of the very environmental problems scripted as threats'. 'It is less the case that famines in Africa in recent decades have produced' so-called 'breeding grounds for conflict', Barnett (2000, 279) continues. 'The more important, pressing and avoidable product is widespread malnutrition and large-scale loss of life'. We concur, and it is for this reason that we wish to bring to the forefront the struc-tural violence and everyday atrocity of environmental destruction.

11 The Darfur conflict cannot be understood without looking also at the deci-sions of the government in Khartoum, the longer-term conflict between Sudan and South Sudan, the dismantling, in the colonial and post-colonial era, of indigenous modes of conflict resolution, and a whole host of other factors (see, e.g., De Waal, 2015).

12 Similarly, drought was a factor in the Syria crisis, although the crisis remained the 'result of complex, interrelated factors' including attempts, by actors within and beyond the region, to stoke ethnic tensions (Gleick, 2014, 331).

13 These changes amplified longer-term trends towards agricultural concentra-tion, which were disadvantageous for small farmers in the global North as well as small farmers in the global South (see, e.g., McMichael, 2009).

14 The G7 refers to the following seven states and the intergovernmental group-ing of them: Canada, France, Germany, Italy, Japan, the UK and the USA.

15 Land can also play a key role in sustaining conflict. In the east of the Democratic Republic of Congo, 'land has turned into a resource of war and of speculation, to the advantage of politico-military elites' (Vlassenroot, 2013, 2). In Darfur, Janjaweed fighters were given the prospect of keeping land that they gained

through war (Abdul-Jalil and Unruh, 2013), and in Rwanda, Hutus involved in land disputes were killed by fellow Hutus in part as a way of acquiring land (Huggins et al., 2005).

16 These reports are not restricted to the African continent: the Indonesian national land agency has confirmed 3,500 land conflicts – not all physically violent – linked to palm oil across the country (Nesadurai, 2013); land conflicts top a list of major grievances cited by Vietnamese people against officials and the government (Hiebert and Nyugen, 2012); and in Papua New Guinea, 'anecdotal evidence suggests that conflicts over land and extractive resource developments are on the rise' (Allen and Monson, 2014, 1).

17 When education was later extended to Hutus, Tutsis were taught in French and Hutus in Kishwahili.

18 Another cable authored by Roebuck (in Naiman, 2015, 305) advises the US government to 'encourage rumours and signals of external plotting' in order to provoke a 'self-defeating over-reaction'.

19 Whilst this report is outlining a series of possible strategies and not explicitly advocating one particular course of action, it indicates that stoking Shia–Sunni tension was very much on the table.

20 We do not make any claims about the motivations of the USA and others. Suggestions include the usual suspects: access to oil and gas (Minim, 2013; Durden, 2012); and worries about the emergence of a regional Shia hegemon after the overthrow of a Sunni leader in Shia-majority Iraq (Hersh, 2007; Nasr, 2006).

21 More than 50 per cent of these weapons were provided by the USA. These weapons included drones, military helicopters, tanks, artillery and aircraft. The overall figure excludes over one million small arms also provided by the USA, 360,000 of which went missing (Holden et al., 2016).

22 The Houthi rebels support the often-marginalised Zaidi Shia Muslim minority in Yemen but also gain support from a wider group of Yemenis frustrated with continued corruption and the slow pace of a transition arrangement.

23 Stavrianakis (2016) argues that, far from restraining arms sales, the arms trade treaty legitimises a liberal form of militarism.

5 Just war and the responsibility to protect in a world of already existing intervention

1 This is not to say that norm dissemination, capacity building and so on are without problems.

2 Brown and Bohm (2016) also criticise the narrow framework of the R2P but respond by *adding* to an otherwise unchanged R2P principles of *jus ante*

bellum (right before war). Similarly, Souter (2016) claims that, in *addition to* protecting through intervention, states can demonstrate their commitment to addressing atrocity by taking in refugees displaced through atrocity crimes. The rest of the R2P framework remains untouched. What seems to follow, then, is further institutionalisation – adding *jus ante bellum* and greater support for refugees. By contrast, we highlight the dangers of leaving the rest of the framework untouched and argue that we need to move towards anti-militarist alternatives to R2P.

3   We are not implying here that if states are considered sufficiently fit, they could then legitimately engage in military intervention. As we have made clear throughout, we object to theorising that fails to engage with the real world but nonetheless gives action-guiding advice. To make claims about what would be justifiable once states have radically changed their practices such that they have become good international citizens would be to engage in such abstraction; it would give action-guiding advice about conduct in a world with which we are not familiar. In addition, our claim here is that states and other international actors have duties to change their harmful practices and assist positively both in the place in which a current atrocity is occurring and elsewhere, where the atrocity of mass avoidable death takes place every day. Correspondingly, when we say that an actor is not fit to intervene by virtue of, say, its arms sales, we don't simply mean that they are unfit to intervene in the places to which they sell weapons. We mean that they are unfit to use the method of war for the purpose of human protection full stop.

4   Mohamed Sahnoun was co-chair of the ICISS.

5   This means that their interventions are unlikely to meet Fabre's (2012, 188–189) test of the justice of humanitarian wars, namely that they must be likely to succeed in 'bringing about the just ends of the intervention with the least amount of wrongful losses to lives and limbs on all sides'. This is not to endorse Fabre's test, but to point out that if she were to think through its implications, she might come to realise that her rights-respecting communities are not legitimate interveners.

6   So, in a twist of irony, it is the pursuit of self-interest which occasionally enables humanitarian warriors to do the morally right thing – by way of engaging in large-scale violence – in order to compensate for their systematic self-interested immoralities in other domains.

7   Hehir (2010) is therefore mistaken when he claims that the R2P is 'sound and fury signifying nothing'; meaningless talk that does not ultimately change anything.

8   As should already be clear, our argument here is that the R2P affects the moral climate of international society, and not that it operates, in a simple

manner, as a Trojan horse (see Brecher, 1987, 184). The R2P does not change structurally the international order. As Brazilian delegates to the Security Council have pointed out, it merely re-states existing international law. The role of the Security Council in deciding on when interventions should take place remains unchanged, and it therefore remains very difficult for states to get multilateral permission to intervene. Russia and/or China are likely to veto proposals to use military means when they suspect that the interests of Western powers are behind calls for intervention, and the USA, France and/ or the UK are likely to veto if they deem, say, Russian interests to be driving calls for intervention (see, e.g., Bellamy, 2015a, 112–133).

9 Stavrianakis (2016) makes this argument in the context of the arms trade treaty.

Concluding remarks: genocide in Rwanda and civil war in Syria

1 The difference in media reporting on Afrin and eastern Ghouta is symp-tomatic of media reporting on the Syrian civil war more broadly. As eastern Aleppo was under siege, US-led coalition forces were re-taking Isis-held Raqqa with enormous civilian casualties. The siege and recapture of Aleppo generated massive public and media outcry at the way in which the Assad regime treated the population. The recapture of Raqqa, by contrast, did not generate a raft of reports on civilian deaths and the destruction of the town. As Cockburn (2018) puts it, 'the role of the international media in the Syrian war has been as partial and misleading as the warring parties inside the country or their foreign sponsors without'.

BIBLIOGRAPHY

Abdul-Jalil, M. and Unruh, J. D. (2013) 'Land rights under stress in Darfur: a volatile dynamic of the conflict', *War & Society*, 32 (2), pp. 156–181.

Abouharb, M. R. and Cingranelli, D. L. (2006) 'The human rights effects of World Bank structural adjustment, 1981–2000', *International Studies Quarterly*, 50 (2), pp. 233–262.

Adano, W. R., Dietz, A. J., Witsenburg, K., and Zaal, A. F. M. (2012) 'Climate change, violent conflict and local institutions in Kenya's drylands', *Journal of Peace Research*, 49 (1), pp. 65–80.

Adekanye, J. B. (1995) 'Structural adjustment, democratization and rising ethnic tensions in Africa', *Development and Change*, 26 (2), pp. 355–374.

African Union (2011) 'Report of the chairperson of the Commission on current challenges to peace and security on the continent and the AU's efforts: enhancing Africa's leadership, promoting African solutions', extraordinary session of the Assembly of the Union on the state of peace and security in Africa, Addis Ababa, 25–26 May 2011.

Al Arabiya (2011) 'Qatar admits it had boots on the ground in Libya', 26 October 2011. Available at: www.alarabiya.net/articles/2011/10/26/173833.html (Accessed: 21 March 2017).

Al Jazeera (2011) 'Gaddafi accepts Chavez talks offer', 03 March 2011. Available at: www.aljazeera.com/%20news/africa/2011/03/20113365739369754.html (Accessed: 21 March 2017).

Al Jazeera (2013) 'Libya Assembly votes for Sharia law', 04 December 2013. Available at: www.aljazeera.com/news/africa/2013/12/libya-assembly-votes-sharia-law-2013124153217603439.html (Accessed: 21 March 2017).

al-Haj, A. (2017) 'Yemen civil war: 10,000 civilians killed and 40,000 injured in conflict, UN reveals', *The Independent*, 17 January 2017. Available at: www.independent.co.uk/news/world/middle-east/yemen-civil-war-civilian-death-toll-10000-killed-40000-injured-conflcit-un-reveals-a7530836.html (Accessed: 21 March 2017).

Allday, L. (2016) 'Controlling the narrative on Syria', *MR Online*, 13 December 2016. Available at: https://mronline.org/2016/12/13/allday131216-html/ (Accessed: 21 March 2017).

Allen, M. and Monson, R. (2014) 'Land and conflict in Papua New Guinea: the role of land mediation', *Security Challenges*, 10 (2), pp. 1–14.

Amnesty International (2012) 'Mali's worst human rights situation in 50 years', Press Release, 16 May 2012. Available at: www.amnesty.org/en/press-releases/2012/05/mali-s-worst-human-rights-situation-50-years/ (Accessed: 21 March 2017).

Anievas, A. and Nişancıoğlu, K. (2016) *How the West came to rule*. London: Pluto Press.

Annan, K. A. (2000) *"We the peoples": the role of the United Nations in the 21st century*. New York: United Nations.

Averre, D. and Davies, L. (2015) 'Russia, humanitarian intervention and the Responsibility to Protect: the case of Syria', *International Affairs*, 91 (4), pp. 813–834.

Axworthy, L. (2011) 'In Libya, we move toward a more humane world', *Globe and Mail*, 23 August 2011. Available at: www.theglobeandmail.com/news/opinions/opinion/in-libya-we-move-toward-a-more-humane-world/article2138221/ (Accessed: 21 March 2017).

Ayoob, M. (2002) 'Inequality and theorizing in international relations: the case for subaltern realism', *International Studies Review*, 4 (3), pp. 27–48.

Baechler, G. (1999) *Violence through environmental discrimination*. Dordrecht: Kluwer Academic Publishers.

Balch-Lindsay, D. and Enterline, A. J. (2000) 'Killing time: the world politics of civil war duration, 1820–1992', *International Studies Quarterly*, 44 (4), pp. 615–642.

Bâli, A. and Rana, A. (2017) 'The wrong kind of intervention in Syria', in Makdisi, K. and Prashad, V. (eds.) *Land of blue helmets: the United Nations in the Arab world*. Oakland, CA: University of California Press, pp. 115–144.

Bannon, I. and Collier, P. (eds.) (2003) *Natural resources and conflict: options and actions*. Washington, DC: The World Bank. Available at: https://openknowledge.worldbank.org/bitstream/handle/10986/15047/282450Naturaloresourcesoviolentoconflict.pdf;sequence=1 (Accessed: 19 August 2018).

Barnett, J. (2000) 'Destabilizing the environment-conflict thesis', *Review of International Studies*, 26 (2), pp. 271–288.

Basham, V. M. (2018) 'Liberal militarism as insecurity, desire and ambivalence: gender, race and the everyday geopolitics of war', *Security Dialogue*, 49 (1–2), pp. 32–43.

Bass, G. B. (2009) *Freedom's battle: the origins of humanitarian intervention*. New York: Alfred A. Knopf.

BBC (2004) 'EU lifts weapons embargo on Libya', 11 October 2004. Available at: http://news.bbc.co.uk/1/hi/3732514.stm (Accessed: 01 November 2017).

BBC (2011a) 'Libya protests: defiant Gaddafi refuses to quit', 22 February 2011. Available at: www.bbc.co.uk/news/world-middle-east-12544624 (Accessed: 01 November 2017).

BBC (2011b) 'A point of view: why euphemism is integral to modern warfare', 19 October 2011. Available at: www.bbc.co.uk/news/magazine-15478001 (Accessed: 20 July 2018).

Bellamy, A. J. (2006) *Just wars: from Cicero to Iraq*. Cambridge: Polity Press.

Bellamy, A. J. (2015a) *The Responsibility to Protect: a defense*. Oxford: Oxford University Press.

Bellamy, A. J. (2015b) 'The Responsibility to Protect turns ten', *Ethics & International Affairs*, 29 (2), pp. 161–185.

Bellamy, A. J. (2016) 'Interview', *Oxford Research Group*, 15 September 2016. Available at: www.oxfordresearchgroup.org.uk/Blog/interview-alex-bellamy (Accessed: 17 August 2018).

Bellamy, A. J. and Williams, P. D. (2011) 'The new politics of protection? Côte d'Ivoire, Libya and the Responsibility to Protect', *International Affairs*, 87 (4), pp. 825–850.

Bellows, A. C., Valente, F. L. S., Lemke, S., and Núñez Burbano de Lara, M. D. (2016) *Gender, nutrition and the human right to adequate food: toward an inclusive framework*. New York: Routledge.

Bennis, P. (2016) 'The war in Syria cannot be won. But it can be ended', *The Nation*, 31 October 2016. Available at: www.thenation.com/article/the-war-in-syria-cannot-be-won-but-it-can-be-ended/ (Accessed: 01 November 2017).

Bigagaza, J., Abong, C., and Mukarubuga, C. (2002) 'Land scarcity, distribution and conflict in Rwanda', in Lind, L. and Sturman, K. (eds.) *Scarcity and surfeit: the ecology of Africa's conflicts*. Pretoria, South Africa: Institute for Security Studies, pp. 51–84.

Black, I. (2011) 'Libyan forces predict fall of rebel-held Benghazi "within 48 hours"', *The Guardian*, 17 March 2011. Available at: www.theguardian.com/world/2011/mar/16/libya-benghazi-gaddafi-48-hours (Accessed: 21 March 2017).

Black, I. (2013) 'Libyan revolution casualties lower than expected, says new government', *The Guardian*, 08 January 2013. Available at: www.theguardian.com/world/2013/jan/08/libyan-revolution-casualties-lower-expected-government (Accessed: 21 March 2017).

Boone, C. (2014) *Property and political order in Africa: land rights and the structure of politics*. New York: Cambridge University Press.

Brantlinger, P. (1988) *Rule of darkness: British literature and imperialism, 1830–1914*. Ithaca, NY: Cornell University Press.

Brecher, B. (1987) 'Surrogacy, liberal individualism and the moral climate', in Evans, S. D. G. (ed.) *Moral philosophy and contemporary problems*. Cambridge: Cambridge University Press, pp. 183–197.

Bricmont, J. (2006) *Humanitarian imperialism: using human rights to sell war*, trans. D. Johnstone. New York: Monthly Review Press.

Brooks, R. (2014) *The great tax robbery: how Britain became a tax haven for fat cats and big business.* London: Oneworld Publications.

Brown, G. W. and Bohm, A. (2016) 'Introducing *jus ante bellum* as a cosmopolitan approach to humanitarian intervention', *European Journal of International Relations,* 22 (4), pp. 897–919.

Bundervoet, T. (2009) 'Livestock, land and political power: the 1993 killings in Burundi', *Journal of Peace Research,* 46 (3), pp. 357–376.

Burnham, G., Lafta, R., Doocy, S., and Roberts, L. (2006) 'Mortality after the 2003 invasion of Iraq: a cross-sectional cluster sample survey', *The Lancet,* 368 (9545), pp. 1421–1428.

Bybee, J. S. (2002) 'Memorandum for Alberto R. Gonzales, Counsel to the President, Re: Standards of Conduct for Interrogation under 18 U.S.C. §§ 2340–2340A', US Department of Justice, Office of Legal Counsel, 01 August 2002. Available at: www.therenditionproject.org.uk/pdf/PDF%2019%20[Bybee%20Memo%20to%20Gonzales%20Standards%20Interrogation%201%20Aug.pdf (Accessed: 18 August 2018).

CAAT – Campaign Against the Arms Trade (2013) 'UK arms sales to Gaddafi's Libya'. Available at: www.caat.org.uk/resources/countries/libya/uk-gaddafi (Accessed: 01 November 2017).

CAAT – Campaign Against the Arms Trade (2017) 'Introduction to the arms trade: human rights abuses'. Available at: www.caat.org.uk/issues/introduction/human-rights (Accessed: 01 November 2017).

Calhoun, L. (2013) *War and delusion: a critical examination.* New York: Palgrave Macmillan.

Campbell, H. (2013) *Global NATO and the catastrophic failure in Libya.* New York: Monthly Review Press.

Carrington, D. (2017) 'Global pollution kills 9m a year and threatens "survival of human societies"', *The Guardian,* 20 October 2017. Available at: www.theguardian.com/environment/2017/oct/19/global-pollution-kills-millions-threatens-survival-human-societies (Accessed: 17 August 2018).

Centre for Applied Research (Norwegian School of Economics), Global Financial Integrity, Jawaharlal Nehru University, Instituto de Estudos Socioeconômicos, Nigerian Institute of Social and Economic Research (2015) 'Financial flows and tax havens: combining to limit the lives of billions of people', December 2015. Washington, DC: Global Financial Integrity. Available at: www.gfintegrity.org/wp-content/uploads/2016/12/Financial_Flows-final.pdf (Accessed: 18 August 2018).

Chang, H.-J. (2002) *Kicking away the ladder: development strategy in historical perspective.* London: Anthem.

Charlesworth, H. (2002) 'International law: a discipline of crisis', *The Modern Law Review*, 65 (3), pp. 377–392.

Charlesworth, H. (2010) 'Feminist reflections on the Responsibility to Protect', *Global Responsibility to Protect*, 2 (3), pp. 232–249.

Chesterman, S. (2001) *Just war or just peace? Humanitarian intervention and international law*. Oxford: Oxford University Press.

Chomsky, N. (2008) 'Humanitarian imperialism: the new doctrine of imperial right', *Monthly Review*, 01 September 2008, pp. 22–50. Available at: https://monthlyreview.org/2008/09/01/humanitarian-imperialism-the-new-doctrine-of-imperial-right/ (Accessed: 17 August 2018).

Clapham, C. (1998) 'Rwanda: the perils of peacemaking', *Journal of Peace Research*, 35 (2), pp. 193–210.

Clapp, J. and Helleiner, E. (2012) 'Troubled futures? The global food crisis and the politics of agricultural derivatives regulation', *Review of International Political Economy*, 19 (2), pp. 181–207.

Clark, D. (2011) 'Which nations are the most responsible for climate change', *The Guardian*, 21 April 2011. Available at: www.theguardian.com/environment/2011/apr/21/countries-responsible-climate-change (Accessed: 17 August 2018).

Climate Vulnerability Forum (2010) 'Climate vulnerability monitor: the state of the climate crisis'. Available at: http://daraint.org/wp-content/uploads/2010/12/CVM_Complete-1-August-2011.pdf (Accessed: 31 October 2017).

CLM – Cunningham Levy Muse (2017) 'Report and recommendation to the Government of Rwanda on the role of French officials in the genocide against the Tutsi', 11 December 2017. Available at: www.cunninghamlevy.com/wp-content/uploads/2017/12/Cunningham-Levy-Muse-Report-to-GOR-2017-12-11.pdf (Accessed: 18 August 2018).

Coates, A. J. (2016) *The ethics of war*. 2nd edn. Manchester: Manchester University Press.

Cockburn, P. (2011) 'Amnesty questions claim that Gaddafi ordered rape as weapon of war', *The Independent*, 24 June 2011. Available at: www.independent.co.uk/news/world/africa/amnesty-questions-claim-that-gaddafi-ordered-rape-as-weapon-of-war-2302037.html (Accessed: 17 August 2018).

Cockburn, P. (2017) 'Who supplies the news? Patrick Cockburn on misreporting in Syria and Iraq', *London Review of Books*, 02 February 2017. Available at: www.lrb.co.uk/v39/n03/patrick-cockburn/who-supplies-the-news (Accessed: 17 August 2018).

Cockburn, P. (2018) 'While the world looks to Eastern Ghouta, civilians in Afrin are being slaughtered in the hundreds by Turkish forces', *The Independent*,

09 March 2018. Available at: www.independent.co.uk/voices/syria-afrin-crisis-turkish-forces-civilians-deaths-eastern-ghouta-assad-a8247206.html (Accessed: 17 August 2018).

Collier, P., Elliott, V. L., Hegre, H., Hoeffler, A., Reynal-Querol, M. and Sambanis, N. (2003) *Breaking the conflict trap: civil war and development policy.* Washington, DC: World Bank and Oxford University Press. Available at: https://openknowledge.worldbank.org/bitstream/handle/10986/13938/567930PUBobrea10Box353739B01PUBLIC1.pdf (Accessed: 19 August 2018).

Comaroff, J. and Comaroff, J. L. (2012) 'Theory from the South: or, how Euro-America is evolving toward Africa', *Anthropological Forum*, 22 (2), pp. 113–131.

Conflict Armament Research (2014) 'Dispatch from the field: Islamic State ammunition in Iraq and Syria', September 2014. London: Conflict Armament Research. Available at: http://conflictarm.com/wp-content/uploads/2014/09/Dispatch_IS_Iraq_Syria_Weapons.pdf (Accessed: 18 August 2018).

Cotula, L. (2014) 'Addressing the human rights impacts of "land grabbing"', Study requested by the European Parliament's Subcommittee on Human Rights, EXPO/B/DROI/2014/06. Available at: www.europarl.europa.eu/RegData/etudes/STUD/2014/534984/EXPO_STU(2014)534984_EN.pdf (Accessed: 31 October 2017).

Coughlin, C. (2011) 'Nato must target Gaddafi regime, says Armed Forces chief Gen Sir David Richards', *The Telegraph*, 14 May 2011. Available at: www.telegraph.co.uk/news/worldnews/africaandindianocean/libya/8514034/Nato-must-target-Gaddafi-regime-says-Armed-Forces-chief-Gen-Sir-David-Richards.html (Accessed: 21 March 2017).

Davis, M. (2002) *Late Victorian holocausts.* London: Verso.

de Alwis, M. (2009) 'Interrogating the "political": feminist peace activism in Sri Lanka', *Feminist Review*, 91, pp. 81–93.

de Schutter, O. (2011) 'How not to think about land grabbing: three critiques of large-scale investments in farmland', *The Journal of Peasant Studies*, 38 (2), pp. 249–279.

de Soysa, I. and Midford, P. (2012) 'Enter the dragon! An empirical analysis of Chinese versus US arms transfers to autocrats and violators of human rights, 1989–2006', *International Studies Quarterly*, 56 (4), pp. 843–856.

de Waal, A. (2013) 'African roles in the Libyan conflict of 2011', *International Affairs*, 89 (2), pp. 365–379.

de Waal, A. (2015) *The real politics of the Horn of Africa: money, war and the business of power.* Cambridge: Polity Press.

Dearden, L. (2017) 'UK weapons companies have made £6bn from Saudi Arabia since it started bombing Yemen', *The Independent*, 19 September 2017. Available at: www.independent.co.uk/news/uk/home-news/yemen-war-saudi-arabia-human-rights-british-weapons-trade-uk-6bn-war-child-report-crimes-civilians-a7953496.html (Accessed: 17 August 2018).

Dehghan, S. K. (2017) 'Global arms trade reaches highest point since Cold War era', *The Guardian*, 20 February 2017. Available at: www.theguardian.com/world/2017/feb/20/global-arms-weapons-trade-highest-point-since-cold-war-era (Accessed: 17 August 2018).

Deininger, K. and Byerlee, D., with Lindsay, J., Norton, A., Selod, H., and Stickler, M. (2011) *Rising global interest in farmland: can it yield sustainable and equitable benefits?* Washington, DC: The World Bank. Available at: https://siteresources.worldbank.org/DEC/Resources/Rising-Global-Interest-in-Farmland.pdf (Accessed: 19 August 2018).

Deng, F. M. (1995) 'Blood brothers', *The Brookings Review*, Summer 1995, pp. 12–17. Available at: www.unz.org/Pub/BrookingsRev-1995q3-00012 (Accessed: 18 August 2018).

Deng, F. M. (2010) 'JISB interview: the Responsibility to Protect', interview by Aidan Hehir, *Journal of Intervention and Statebuilding*, 4 (1), pp. 83–89.

Deng, F. M., Kimaro, S., Lyons, T., Rothchild, D., and Zartman, I. W. (1996) *Sovereignty as responsibility: conflict management in Africa.* Washington, DC: The Brookings Institution.

Doss, C., Summerfield, G. and Tsikata, D. (2014) 'Land, gender, and food security', *Feminist Economics*, 20 (1), pp. 1–23.

Dower, N. (2009) *The ethics of war and peace.* Cambridge: Polity.

DS – Do Something (2017) '11 facts about global poverty'. Available at: www.dosomething.org/us/facts/11-facts-about-global-poverty (Accessed: 31 October 2017).

Dunford, R. (2016) *The politics of transnational peasant struggle: resistance, rights and democracy.* London: Rowman & Littlefield International.

Dunford, R. (2017) 'Toward a decolonial global ethics', *Journal of Global Ethics*, 13 (3), pp. 1–18.

Dunne, T. and Gelber, K. (2014) 'Arguing matters: the Responsibility to Protect and the case of Libya', *Global Responsibility to Protect*, 6 (3), pp. 326–349.

Dunne, T. and Gelber, K. (2015) 'Text and context in the Responsibility to Protect: a reply to Hehir', *Global Responsibility to Protect*, 7 (2), pp. 225–233.

Durden, T. (2012) 'Presenting the Russian naval base in Tartus, Syria, or good luck UN Security Council', *Zero Hedge*, 02 April 2012. Available at: www.zerohedge.com/news/presenting-russian-naval-base-tartus-syria-or-good-luck-un-security-council (Accessed: 17 August 2018).

Dussel, E. D. (1995) *The invention of the Americas: eclipse of "the other" and the myth of modernity*, trans. M. D. Barber. New York: Continuum.

ECFR – European Council on Foreign Relations (2016) 'A quick guide to Libya's main players'. Available at: www.ecfr.eu/mena/mapping_libya_conflict (Accessed: 21 March 2017).

Edward, P. (2006) 'The ethical poverty line: a moral quantification of absolute poverty', *Third World Quarterly*, 27 (2), pp. 377–393.

Engle, K. (2007) '"Calling in the troops": the uneasy relationship among women's rights, human rights, and humanitarian intervention', *Harvard Human Rights Journal*, 20, pp. 189–226.

Enloe, C. H. (2007) *Globalization and militarism: feminists make the link*. 2nd edn. Lanham, MD: Rowman & Littlefield.

Eschle, C. (2017) 'Beyond Greenham woman? Gender identities and anti-nuclear activism in peace camps', *International Feminist Journal of Politics*, 19 (4), pp. 471–490.

Escobar, A. (1995) *Encountering development: the making and unmaking of the Third World*. Princeton, NJ: Princeton University Press.

Espinoza, M. and Afxentiou, A. (2018) 'Editor's introduction: drones and state terrorism', *Critical Studies on Terrorism*, 11 (2), pp. 295–300.

EU Parliament (2016) 'Paper on the New Alliance for Food Security and Nutrition', Committee on Development, Procedure 2015/2277 (INI), 03 May 2016. Available at: www.europarl.europa.eu/sides/getDoc.do?pubRef=-//EP//TEXT+REPORT+A8-2016-0169+0+DOC+XML+V0//EN (Accessed: 17 August 2018).

Eurostat (2017) 'Statistics explained: amenable and preventable deaths statistics'. Available at: http://ec.europa.eu/eurostat/statistics-explained/index.php/Amenable_and_preventable_deaths_statistics (Accessed: 31 October 2017).

Evans, G. (2009) *The Responsibility to Protect: ending mass atrocity crimes once and for all*. Washington, DC: Brookings Institution Press.

Evans, G. (2011) 'Interview: the R2P balance sheet after Libya', in T. G. Weiss et al., *The Responsibility to Protect: challenges and opportunities in light of the Libyan intervention*, November 2011, pp. 34–42. Available at: www.e-ir.info/wp-content/uploads/R2P.pdf (Accessed: 17 August 2017).

Evans, G. (2012) 'Gareth Evans on "Responsibility to Protect" after Libya', interview by Alan Philps, *The World Today*, 68 (5), 05 October 2012. Available at: www.chathamhouse.org/publications/twt/archive/view/186279 (Accessed: 18 July 2018).

Evans, M. (2005) 'Moral theory and the idea of a just war', in Evans, M. (ed.) *Just war theory: a reappraisal*. Edinburgh: Edinburgh University Press, pp. 1–21.

Fabre, C. (2012) *Cosmopolitan war*. Oxford: Oxford University Press.

Fairhead, J., Leach, M., and Scoones, I. (2012) 'Green grabbing: a new appropriation of nature?' *Journal of Peasant Studies*, 39 (2), pp. 237–261.

FAO, IFAD, UNICEF, WFP, and WHO (2012) 'The state of food security and nutrition in the world: economic growth is necessary but not sufficient to accelerate reduction of hunger and malnutrition'. Rome: FAO. Available at: www.fao.org/docrep/016/i3027e/i3027e.pdf (Accessed: 19 August 2018).

FAO, IFAD, UNICEF, WFP, and WHO (2017) 'The state of food security and nutrition in the world: building resilience for peace and security'. Rome: FAO. Available at: www.fao.org/3/a-I7695e.pdf (Accessed: 19 August 2018).

Farer, T. J. (1996) 'Intervention in unnatural humanitarian emergencies: lessons of the first phase', *Human Rights Quarterly*, 18 (1), pp. 1–22.

Fearon, J. D. and Laitin, D. D. (2003) 'Ethnicity, insurgency, and civil war', *The American Political Science Review*, 97 (1), pp. 75–90.

Fildis, A. T. (2011) 'The troubles in Syria: spawned by French divide and rule', *Middle East Policy*, 18 (4), pp. 129–139.

Finnemore, M. and Sikkink, K. (1998) 'International norm dynamics and political change', *International Organization*, 52 (4), pp. 887–917.

Fisher, D. (2011) *Morality and war: can war be just in the twenty-first century?* Oxford: Oxford University Press.

Flint, J. (2009) 'Beyond "Janjaweed": understanding the militias of Darfur', Small Arms Survey, Geneva, Graduate Institute of International and Development Studies. Available at: www.smallarmssurveysudan.org/fileadmin/docs/working-papers/HSBA-WP-17-Beyond-Janjaweed.pdf (Accessed: 18 January 2018).

Fortna, V. P. (2008) *Does peacekeeping work? Shaping belligerents' choices after civil war*. Princeton, NJ: Princeton University Press.

Frank, A. G. (1966) *The development of underdevelopment*. Boston, MA: New England Free Press.

Frowe, H. (2011) *The ethics of war and peace: an introduction*. Abingdon: Routledge.

Galeano, E. (2009) *Open veins of Latin America: five centuries of the pillage of a continent*. London: Profile Books.

Galtung, J. (1969) 'Violence, peace, and peace research', *Journal of Peace Research*, 6 (3), pp. 167–191.

Galtung, J. (1990) 'Cultural violence', *Journal of Peace Research*, 27 (3), pp. 291–305.

Gleick, P. H. (2014) 'Water, drought, climate change, and conflict in Syria', *American Meteorological Society*, 6 (3), pp. 331–340.

Global Witness (2013) 'Rubber barons: how Vietnamese companies and international financiers are driving a land grabbing crisis in Cambodia and Laos'. London: Global Witness.

Graubart, J. (2013) 'R2P and pragmatic liberal interventionism: values in the service of interests', *Human Rights Quarterly*, 35 (1), pp. 69–90.

Guardian (2011) 'EU arms exports to Libya: who armed Gaddafi?' 01 March 2011. Available at: www.theguardian.com/news/datablog/2011/mar/01/eu-arms-exports-libya (Accessed: 17 August 2018).

Gürcan, E. C. (2014) 'Cuban agriculture and food sovereignty: beyond civil-society-centric and globalist paradigms', *Latin American Perspectives*, 41 (4), pp. 129–146.

Hafner-Burton, E. M. (2014) 'A social science of human rights', *Journal of Peace Research*, 51 (2), pp. 273–286.

Hallam, R. (2016) 'Climate change, racism, and black lives', *openDemocracy UK*, 27 September 2016. Available at: www.opendemocracy.net/uk/roger-hallam/climate-change-racism-and-black-lives (Accessed: 17 August 2018).

Hauge, W. I. and Ellingsen, T. (1998) 'Beyond environmental scarcity: causal pathways to conflict', *Journal of Peace Research*, 35 (3), pp. 299–317.

HCFAC – House of Commons Foreign Affairs Committee (2016) 'Libya: examination of intervention and collapse and the UK's future policy options', Third Report of Session 2016–17. Available at: www.publications.parliament.uk/pa/cm201617/cmselect/cmfaff/119/119.pdf (Accessed: 21 March 2017).

Heathcote, G. (2014) 'Feminist perspectives on the law on the use of force', in Weller, M. (ed.) *The Oxford Handbook of the Use of Force in International Law*. Oxford: Oxford University Press, pp. 114–128.

Hehir, A. (2010) 'The Responsibility to Protect: "sound and fury signifying nothing"?' *International Relations*, 24 (2), pp. 218–239.

Hehir, A. (2013) 'The permanence of inconsistency: Libya, the Security Council, and the Responsibility to Protect', *International Security*, 38 (1), pp. 137–159.

Hehir, A. (2015) 'The dog that didn't bark? A response to Dunne and Gelber's analysis of RtoP's influence on the intervention in Libya', *Global Responsibility to Protect*, 7 (2), pp. 211–224.

Hehir, A. (2016) 'Libya's collapse into chaos is not an argument against intervention', *The Conversation*, 27 April 2016. Available at: http://theconversation.com/libyas-collapse-into-chaos-is-not-an-argument-against-intervention-57776 (Accessed: 17 August 2018).

Heinbecker, P. (2011) 'Plenty of credit to go around in Gadhafi's fall', *Center for International Governance Innovation*, 23 August 2011. Available at:

www.cigionline.org/articles/plenty-credit-go-around-gadhafis-fall (Accessed: 17 August 2018).

Heller, H. (2006) *The Cold War and imperialism*. New York: Monthly Review Press.

Hersh, S. M. (2007) 'The Redirection: is the administration's new policy benefitting our enemies in the war on terrorism?' *The New Yorker*, 05 March 2007. Available at: www.newyorker.com/magazine/2007/03/05/the-redirection (Accessed: 17 August 2008).

Hickel, J. (2013) '"The donors' dilemma" – aid in reverse: how poor countries develop rich countries', *Global Policy Journal*, 12 December 2013. Available at: www.globalpolicyjournal.com/blog/12/12/2013/donors%E2%80%99-dilemma-aid-reverse-how-poor-countries-develop-rich-countries (Accessed: 20 July 2018).

Hickel, J. (2016) 'The true extent of global poverty and hunger: questioning the good news narrative of the Millennium Development Goals', *Third World Quarterly*, 37 (5), pp. 749–767.

Hickel, J. (2017) *The divide: a brief guide to global inequality and its solutions*. London: William Heinemann.

Hiebert, M. and Nyugen, P. (2012) 'Land disputes stir political debate in Vietnam', Center for Strategic and International Studies, 24 July 2012. Available at: www.csis.org/analysis/land-disputes-stir-political-debate-vietnam (Accessed: 18 August 2018).

Higgins, P. (2015) 'The war on Syria', *Jacobin Magazine*, 27 August 2015. Available at: www.jacobinmag.com/2015/08/syria-civil-war-nato-military-intervention/ (Accessed: 17 August, 2018).

Hippler, J. (1995) 'Democratisation of the third world after the end of the Cold War', in Hippler, J. (ed.) *The democratisation of disempowerment: the problem of democracy in the third world*. London: Pluto Press, pp. 1–31.

Holden, P., Detzner, S., Conley-Zilkic, B., de Waal, A., Dunne, J., Feinstein, A., Hartung, W., Holtom, P., Lumpe, L., Marsh, N., Perlo-Freeman, S., van Vuuren, H., and Wawro, L. (2016) *Indefensible: seven myths that sustain the global arms trade*. London: Zed.

Holmes, J. (2014) 'Responsibility to Protect: a humanitarian overview', *Global Responsibility to Protect*, 6 (2), pp. 126–145.

Holt, V. K. and Berkman, T. C. (2006) *The impossible mandate? Military as preparedness, the Responsibility to Protect and modern peace operations*. Washington, DC: Henry L. Stimson Center.

Holt-Giménez, E. (2009) 'From food crisis to food sovereignty: the challenge of social movements', *Monthly Review* 61 (3), pp. 142–156.

Holt-Giménez, E., Shattuck, A., Altieri, M., Herren, H., and Gliessman, S. (2012) 'We already grow enough food for 10 billion people ... and still can't end hunger', *Journal of Sustainable Agriculture*, 36 (6), pp. 595–598.

Homer-Dixon, T. F. and Blitt, J. (eds.) (1998) *Ecoviolence: links among environment, population, and security*. Lanham, MD: Rowman & Littlefield.

Hopgood, S. (2014) 'The last rites for humanitarian intervention: Darfur, Sri Lanka and *R2P*', *Global Responsibility to Protect*, 6 (2), pp. 181–205.

Huggins, C., Musahara, H., Kamungi, P. M., Oketch, J. S., and Vlassenroot, K. (2005) 'Conflict in the Great Lakes region: how is it linked with land and migration?' *Natural Resource Perspectives*, 96. Available at: www.odi. org/sites/odi.org.uk/files/odi-assets/publications-opinion-files/2352.pdf (Accessed: 18 August 2018).

Human Rights Watch (2011) 'Libya: government attacks in Misrata kill civilians: unlawful strike on medical clinic', 10 April 2011. Available at: www.hrw. org/news/2011/04/10/libya-government-attacks-misrata-kill-civilians (Accessed: 18 August 2018).

Human Rights Watch (2012a) 'Unacknowledged deaths: civilian casualties in NATO's air campaign in Libya', May 2012. Available at: https://reliefweb.int/ sites/reliefweb.int/files/resources/libya0512webwcover.pdf (Accessed: 18 August 2018).

Human Rights Watch (2012b) 'Libya: wake-up call to Misrata's leaders: torture, killings may amount to crimes against humanity', 08 April 2012. Available at: www. hrw.org/news/2012/04/08/libya-wake-call-misratas-leaders (Accessed: 21 March 2017).

Human Rights Watch (2016) 'Yemen: US bombs used in deadliest market strike: coalition should stop selling weapons to Saudi Arabia', 07 April 2016. Available at: www.hrw.org/news/2016/04/07/yemen-us-bombs-used-deadliest-market-strike (Accessed: 21 March 2017).

Human Rights Watch (2017) 'Yemen: events of 2016'. Available at: www.hrw.org/ world-report/2017/country-chapters/yemen (Accessed: 18 August 2018).

Hunger and World Poverty (2017) 'Hunger and world poverty'. Available at: www. poverty.com (Accessed: 31 October 2017).

ICISS – International Commission on Intervention and State Sovereignty (2001) 'The Responsibility to Protect', Canada: International Development Research Centre. Available at: http://responsibilitytoprotect.org/ICISS%20 Report.pdf (Accessed: 18 August 2018).

Ide, T. (2017) 'Research methods for exploring the links between climate change and conflict', *Wiley Interdisciplinary Reviews: Climate Change*, 8 (3), pp. 1–14.

Ignatius, D. (2012) 'Libyan weapons on the loose', *Washington Post*, 9 May 2012. Available at: www.washingtonpost.com/gdpr-consent/?destination =%2fopinions%2flibyan-missiles-on-the-loose%2f2012%2f05%2f08%2fgl QA1FCUBU_story.html%3f&utm_term=.1a445c62df45 (Accessed: 21 March 2017).

International Crisis Group (2011) 'Popular protest in North Africa and the Middle East (V): making sense of Libya', Report No. 107, Middle East and North Africa Report. Available at: www.crisisgroup.org/middle-east-north-africa/ north-africa/libya/popular-protest-north-africa-and-middle-east-v-making-sense-libya (Accessed: 18 August 2018).

Jonas, S. (1991) *The battle for Guatemala: rebels, death squads, and U.S. power.* Boulder, CO: Westview Press.

Junk, J. (2016) 'Testing boundaries: cyclone Nargis in Myanmar and the scope of R2P', *Global Society*, 30 (1), pp. 78–93.

Justin, P. H. and van Leeuwen, M. (2016) 'The politics of displacement-related land conflict in Yei River County, South Sudan', *The Journal of Modern African Studies*, 54 (3), pp. 419–442.

Kahl, C. H. (2006) *States, scarcity, and civil strife in the developing world.* Princeton, NJ: Princeton University Press.

Kamm, F. (2012) *The moral target: aiming at right conduct in war and other conflicts.* Oxford: Oxford University Press.

Kamola, I. A. (2007) 'The global coffee economy and the production of genocide in Rwanda', *Third World Quarterly*, 28 (3), pp. 571–592.

Kaplan, R. D. (2001) *The coming anarchy: shattering the dreams of the post Cold War.* New York: Vintage.

Karp, D. J. (2015) 'The responsibility to protect human rights and the RtoP: prospective and retrospective responsibility', *Global Responsibility to Protect*, 7 (2), pp. 142–166.

Kelbert, A. W. (2016) 'Climate change is a racist crisis: that's why Black Lives Matter closed an airport', *The Guardian*, 06 September 2016. Available at: www.theguardian.com/commentisfree/2016/sep/06/climate-change-racist-crisis-london-city-airport-black-lives-matter (Accessed: 19 August 2018).

Kelly, A. B. (2011) 'Conservation practice as primitive accumulation', *The Journal of Peasant Studies*, 38 (4), pp. 683–701.

Kennedy, D. (2006) 'Modern war and modern law', speech given at the Watson Institute, Brown University, 12 October 2006. Available at: www.law. harvard.edu/faculty/dkennedy/speeches/BrownWarSpeech.pdf (Accessed: 18 August 2018).

Khalili, L. (2012) *Time in the shadows.* Stanford, CA: Stanford University Press.

ki-Moon, B. (2007) 'A climate culprit in Darfur', *Washington Post*, 15 June 2007. Available at: www.washingtonpost.com/wp-dyn/content/article/2007/06/15/AR2007061501857.html (Accessed: 17 August 2018).

ki-Moon, B. (2011) 'Remarks at breakfast roundtable with foreign ministers', United Nations Secretary-General, 23 September 2011. Available at: www.un.org/sg/en/content/sg/speeches/2011-09-23/remarks-breakfast-roundtable-foreign-ministers-responsibility-protect (Accessed: 22 December 2016).

Krain, M. (2005) 'International intervention and the severity of genocides and politicides', *International Studies Quarterly*, 49 (3), pp. 363–388.

Krause, V. and Suzuki, S. (2005) 'Causes of civil war in Asia and sub-Saharan Africa: a comparison', *Social Science Quarterly*, 86 (1), pp. 160–177.

Kuperman, A. J. (2013) 'A model humanitarian intervention? Reassessing NATO's Libya campaign', *International Security*, 38 (1), pp. 105–136.

Lancet Commission on Pollution and Health (2017) 'The Lancet Commission on pollution and health', *The Lancet*, 391 (10119). Available at: www.thelancet.com/commissions/pollution-and-health (Accessed: 18 August 2018).

Lango, J. W. (2014) *The ethics of armed conflict: a cosmopolitan just war theory*. Edinburgh: Edinburgh University Press.

Lazar, S. (2017) 'War', *The Stanford encyclopedia of philosophy*, ed. E. N. Zalta. Available at: https://plato.stanford.edu/archives/spr2017/entries/war/ (Accessed: 19 August 2018).

Lederer, E. M. (2013) 'UN Panel: Libyan weapons spread at alarming rate', *Times of Israel*, 10 April 2013. Available at: www.timesofisrael.com/un-panel-libyan-weapons-spread-at-alarming-rate/ (Accessed: 17 August 2018).

Leech, G. (2012) *Capitalism: a structural genocide*. London: Zed.

Liberti, S. (2013) *Land grabbing: journeys in the new colonialism*. London: Verso.

Loiselle, M.-E. (2013) 'The normative status of the Responsibility to Protect after Libya', *Global Responsibility to Protect*, 5 (3), pp. 317–341.

Luck, E. C. (2011a) 'The Responsibility to Protect: the first decade', *Global Responsibility to Protect*, 3 (4), pp. 387–399.

Luck, E. C. (2011b) 'Interview with Edward Luck, Special Advisor to the Secretary-General', *UN News Centre*, 01 August 2011. Available at: www.un.org/apps/news/newsmakers.asp?NewsID=38 (Accessed: 22 December 2016).

Lugones, M. (2010) 'Toward a decolonial feminism', *Hypatia*, 25 (4), pp. 742–759.

Mahjar-Barducci, A. (2014) 'Libya: the Islamization of universities', *Gatestone Institute*, 14 May 2014. Available at: www.gatestoneinstitute.org/4316/libya-islamization-universities (Accessed: 21 March 2017).

Mamdani, M. (1996) *Citizens and subjects: contemporary Africa and the legacy of late colonialism*. Princeton, NJ: Princeton University Press.

Mamdani, M. (2002) *When victims become killers: colonialism, nativism, and the genocide in Rwanda.* Princeton, NJ: Princeton University Press.

Mamdani, M. (2009) *Saviours and survivors: Darfur, politics, and the war on terror.* Cape Town: HSRC Press.

Mamdani, M. (2010) 'Responsibility to Protect or right to punish?' *Journal of Intervention and Statebuilding,* 4 (1), pp. 53–67.

Mani, R. and Weiss, T. G. (2011) 'R2P's missing link, culture', *Global Responsibility to Protect,* 3 (4), pp. 451–472.

Mann, M. (1987) 'The roots and contradictions of modern militarism', *New Left Review,* 162, pp. 35–50.

Martínez-Torres, E. and Rosset, P. (2010) 'La Vía Campesina: the birth and evolution of a transnational social movement', *The Journal of Peasant Studies,* 37 (1), pp. 149–175.

May, L. (2008) *Aggression and crimes against peace.* Cambridge: Cambridge University Press.

May, T. (2015) *Nonviolent resistance: a philosophical introduction.* Cambridge: Polity Press.

McMahan, J. (2004) 'War as self-defense', *Ethics and International Affairs,* 18 (1), pp. 75–80.

McMahan, J. (2009) *Killing in war.* Oxford: Clarendon Press.

McMichael, P. (2009) 'A food regime genealogy', *The Journal of Peasant Studies,* 36 (1), pp. 139–169.

Melvern, L. (2006) *Conspiracy to murder: the Rwandan genocide.* London and New York: Verso.

Meo, N. (2011) 'Libya: Jacob Zuma accuses Nato of not sticking to UN resolution', *The Telegraph,* 14 June 2011. Available at: www.telegraph.co.uk/news/worldnews/africaandindianocean/libya/8575984/Libya-Jacob-Zuma-accuses-Nato-of-not-sticking-to-UN-resolution.html (Accessed: 18 August 2018).

Mignolo, W. (2011) *The darker side of Western modernity: global futures, decolonial options.* Durham, NC and London: Duke University Press.

Millar, G. (2016) 'Local experiences of liberal peace', *Journal of Peace Research,* 53 (4), pp. 569–581.

Miller, G. (2012) 'Assessing al-Qaeda a year after bin Laden', *Washington Post,* 29 April 2012. Available at: www.pressreader.com/usa/the-washington-post-sunday/20120429/281500748258970 (Accessed: 21 March 2017).

Mills, K. and O'Driscoll, C. (2010) 'From humanitarian intervention to the Responsibility to Protect', *The International Studies Encyclopedia.* London: Wiley-Blackwell, pp. 2532–2552.

Milne, S. (2011) 'If the Libyan war was about saving lives, it was a catastrophic failure', *The Guardian*, 26 October 2011. Available at: www.theguardian.com/commentisfree/2011/oct/26/libya-war-saving-lives-catastrophic-failure (Accessed: 21 March 2017).

Minim, D. (2013) 'The geopolitics of gas and the Syrian crisis', *Strategic Culture*, 31 May 2013. Available at: www.strategic-culture.org/news/2013/05/31/the-geopolitics-of-gas-and-the-syrian-crisis.html (Accessed: 17 August 2018).

Mohamed, R. (2017) 'The UK has made 10 times more in arms sales to Saudi Arabia than it's given in aid to Yemen', *The Independent*, 22 March 2017. Available at: www.independent.co.uk/voices/saudi-arabia-arms-sales-yemen-war-uk-government-us-donald-trump-obama-aid-a7643066.html (Accessed: 17 August 2018).

Mohamed, S. (2012) 'Taking stock of the Responsibility to Protect', *Stanford Journal of International Law*, 48 (2), pp. 319–339.

Moore, J. (2017) 'Rwanda accuses France of complicity in 1994 genocide', *The New York Times*, 13 December 2017. Available at: www.nytimes.com/2017/12/13/world/africa/rwanda-france-genocide.html (Accessed: 17 August 2018).

Müller, H. and Wolff, J. (2014) 'The dual use of an historical event: "Rwanda 1994", the justification and critique of liberal interventionism', *Journal of Intervention and Statebuilding*, 8 (4), pp. 280–290.

Murray, R. W. and Hehir, A. (2012) 'Intervention in the emerging multipolar system: why R2P will miss the unipolar moment', *Journal of Intervention and Statebuilding*, 6 (4), pp. 387–406.

Naiman, R. (2015) 'Syria', in *The Wikileaks Files*. London: Verso, pp. 297–322.

Nasr, V. (2006) 'When the Shiites rise', *Foreign Affairs*, July/August 2006. Available at: www.foreignaffairs.com/articles/iran/2006-07-01/when-shiites-rise (Accessed: 17 August 2018).

Nesadurai, H. E. S. (2013) 'Food security, the palm oil–land conflict nexus, and sustainability: a governance role for a private multi-stakeholder regime like the RSPO?' *The Pacific Review*, 26 (5), pp. 505–529.

Nesbitt, F. N. (2012) 'Principled intervention in Africa: the recent ICC indictment of four Kenyans represents a model for international involvement in conflict resolution in Africa', *Foreign Policy in Focus*, 02 February 2012. Available at: https://fpif.org/principled_intervention_in_africa/ (Accessed: 17 August 2018).

Neu, M. (2017) *Just liberal violence: sweatshops, torture, war.* London: Rowman & Littlefield International.

Nhantumbo, I. and Salomão, A. (2010) 'Biofuels, land access and rural livelihoods in Mozambique', London: International Institute for Environment and Development. Available at: http://pubs.iied.org/pdfs/12563IIED.pdf (Accessed: 01 November 2017).

Nili, S. (2011) 'Humanitarian disintervention', *Journal of Global Ethics*, 7 (1), pp. 33–46.

Nolte, K., Chamberlain, W., and Giger, M. (2016) *International land deals for agriculture: fresh insights from the land matrix: analytical report II.* Bern, Montpellier, Hamburg and Pretoria: Centre for Development and Environment, University of Bern. Available at: https://landmatrix.org/media/filer_public/ab/c8/abc8b563-9d74-4a47-9548-cb59e4809b4e/land_matrix_2016_analytical_report_draft_ii.pdf (Accessed: 18 August 2018).

Norris, J. (2005) *Collision course.* Westport, CT: Praeger.

O'Connell, M. E. (2010) 'Responsibility to peace: a critique of R2P', *Journal of Intervention and Statebuilding*, 4 (1), pp. 39–52.

Oakland Institute (2011) 'Understanding land investment deals in Africa: land grabs leave Africa thirsty', Land Brief Deal, December 2011. Available at: www.oaklandinstitute.org/sites/oaklandinstitute.org/files/OI_brief_land_grabs_leave_africa_thirsty_1.pdf (Accessed: 17 August 2018).

Oakland Institute (2012) 'Understanding land investment deals in Africa: massive deforestation portrayed as sustainable development: the deceit of Herakles farms in Cameroon'. Oakland, CA: The Oakland Institute. Available at: www.oaklandinstitute.org/sites/oaklandinstitute.org/files/Land_deal_brief_herakles.pdf (Accessed: 18 August 2018).

Oakland Institute (2014) 'Engineering ethnic conflict: the toll of Ethiopia's plantation development on the Suri People'. Oakland, CA: The Oakland Institute. Available at: www.oaklandinstitute.org/sites/oaklandinstitute.org/files/Report_EngineeringEthnicConflict.pdf (Accessed: 18 August 2018).

Obama, B. (2016) 'President Obama's interview with Jeffrey Goldberg on Syria and foreign policy', *The Atlantic*, 13 March 2016. Available at: www.theatlantic.com/magazine/archive/2016/04/the-obama-doctrine/471525/ (Accessed: 17 August 2018).

OHCHR – United Nations Office of the High Commissioner for Human Rights (2012) 'Human Rights Council: report of the International Commission of Inquiry on Libya', advanced unedited version, 08 March 2012. Available at: www.ohchr.org/Documents/HRBodies/HRCouncil/RegularSession/Session19/A.HRC.19.68.pdf (Accessed: 18 August 2018).

OHCHR – United Nations Office of the High Commissioner for Human Rights (2015) 'Report on the human rights situation in Libya', 16 November 2015. Available at: www.ohchr.org/Documents/Countries/LY/UNSMIL_OHCHRJointly_report_Libya_16.11.15.pdf (Accessed: 18 August 2018).

Ohlsson, L. (2000) 'Livelihood conflicts: linking poverty and environment as causes of conflict', Swedish International Development Agency, December 2000. Available at: www.sida.se/contentassets/99c24545bf31484aa0e6bbd7658a5873/

livelihood-conflicts-linking-poverty-and-environment-as-causes-of-conflict_1326.pdf (Accessed: 18 August 2010).

Orend, B. (2013) *The morality of war*. 2nd edn. Peterborough, Ontario: Broadview Press.

Orford, A. (1997) 'Locating the international: military and monetary interventions after the Cold War', *Harvard International Law Journal*, 38 (2), pp. 443–486.

Orford, A. (1999) 'Muscular humanitarianism: reading the narratives of the new interventionism', *European Journal of International Law*, 10 (4), pp. 679–711.

Orford, A. (2003) *Reading humanitarian intervention: human rights and the use of force in international law*. Cambridge: Cambridge University Press.

Orford, A. (2011) *International authority and the Responsibility to Protect*. Cambridge: Cambridge University Press.

Osbourne, S. (2016) 'Cameron refuses to launch inquiry into arms sales to Saudi Arabia', *The Independent*, 27 January 2016. Available at: www.independent. co.uk/news/uk/politics/cameron-refuses-to-launch-inquiry-into-arms-sales-to-saudi-arabia-a6836601.html (Accessed: 01 November 2017).

Oxfam (2011) 'Land and power: the growing scandal surrounding the new wave of investments in land'. Oxford: Oxfam. Available at: https:// oxfamilibrary.openrepository.com/bitstream/handle/10546/142858/ bp151-land-power-rights-acquisitions-220911-en.pdf;jsessionid=55 FDA8FB8C2CED0B912959E1FA5637F2?sequence=32 (Accessed: 18 August 2017).

Oxfam (2018) 'Richest 1 percent bagged 82 percent of wealth created last year – poorest half of humanity got nothing', 22 January 2018. Available at: www. oxfam.org/en/pressroom/pressreleases/2018-01-22/richest-1-percent-bagged-82-percent-wealth-created-last-year (Accessed: 18 August 2018).

Paris, R. (2002) 'International peacebuilding and the "mission civilisatrice"', *Review of International Studies*, 28 (4), pp. 637–656.

Paris, R. (2010) 'Saving liberal peacebuilding', *Review of International Studies*, 36 (2), pp. 337–365.

Paris, R. (2014) 'The "Responsibility to Protect" and the structural problems of preventive humanitarian intervention', *International Peacekeeping*, 21 (5), pp. 569–603.

Parliament (2012) 'Arms export controls 2013', Session 2012–13, Submission from Andrew Feinstein, with research by Barnaby Pace, [both of Corruption Watch UK] to the Committees on Arms Export Controls. Available at: https:// publications.parliament.uk/pa/cm201213/cmselect/cmquad/writev/689/ mo3.htm (Accessed: 18 August 2018).

Patel, R. (2008) *Stuffed and starved: the hidden battle for the world food system*. London: Portobello Books.

Peksen, D. (2012) 'Does foreign military intervention help human rights?' *Political Research Quarterly*, 65 (3), pp. 558–571.

Pergantis, V. (2014) 'Strange bedfellows: exploring the relationship between R2P and art. 4(h) of the AU Constitutive Act with regard to military intervention', *Global Responsibility to Protect*, 6 (3), pp. 295–325.

Perkins, R. and Neumayer, E. (2010) 'The organized hypocrisy of ethical foreign policy: human rights, democracy and Western arms sales', *Geoforum*, 41 (2), pp. 247–256.

Pernin, C. G., Nichiporuk, B., Stahl, D., Beck, J., and Radaelli-Sanchez, R. (2008) *Unfolding the future of the long war: motivations, prospects, and implications for the U.S. army.* Santa Monica, CA: RAND Corporation. Available at: www.rand.org/content/dam/rand/pubs/monographs/2008/RAND_MG738.sum.pdf (Accessed: 19 August 2018).

Peters, P. E. (2013) 'Land appropriation, surplus people and a battle over visions of agrarian futures in Africa', *The Journal of Peasant Studies*, 40 (3), pp. 537–562.

Pettersson, T. and Wallensteen, P. (2015) 'Armed conflicts, 1946–2014', *Journal of Peace Research*, 52 (4), pp. 536–550.

Phillips, C. (2015) 'Sectarianism and conflict in Syria', *Third World Quarterly*, 36 (2), pp. 357–376.

Pourmokhtari, N. (2013) 'A postcolonial critique of state sovereignty in IR: the contradictory legacy of a "West-centric" discipline', *Third World Quarterly*, 34 (10), pp. 1767–1793.

Power, S. (2001) 'Bystanders to genocide: why the United States let the Rwandan tragedy happen', *The Atlantic Monthly*, September 2001, pp. 84–108. Available at: https://web.stanford.edu/~sstedman/2006.readings/bystanders.pdf (Accessed: 17 August 2018).

Pritchard, B. (2009) 'The long hangover from the second food regime: a world-historical interpretation of the collapse of the WTO Doha Round', *Agriculture and Human Values*, 26 (4), pp. 297–307.

Quijano, A. (2007) 'Coloniality and modernity/rationality', *Cultural Studies*, 21 (2/3), pp. 168–178.

Quinton-Brown, P. (2013) 'Mapping dissent: the Responsibility to Protect and its state critics', *Global Responsibility to Protect*, 5 (3), pp. 260–282.

Rengger, N. (2013) *Just war and international order: the uncivil condition of world politics.* Cambridge: Cambridge University Press.

Reuters (2012) 'Analyst says Somali pirates have new weapons from Libya', 12 April 2012. Available at: www.reuters.com/article/us-africa-pirates/analyst-says-somali-pirates-have-new-weapons-from-libya-idUSBRE83BoHO20120412 (Accessed: 21 March 2017).

Rights Watch UK (2017) 'Court ruling dismisses the challenge to halt UK arms sales to Saudi Arabia', 10 July 2017. Available at: www.rwuk.org/court-ruling-that-arms-sales-to-saudi-arabia-are-lawful-gives-uk-government-green-light-to-continue-to-prioritise-a-strategic-relationship-and-financial-gain-over-the-lives-of-yemen/ (Accessed: 19 August 2018).

Roberts, A. (1999) 'NATO's humanitarian war over Kosovo', *Survival*, 41 (3), pp. 102–123.

Rodney, W. (2012) *How Europe underdeveloped Africa*. Cape Town: Pambazuka Press.

Rossdale, C. (forthcoming) *Resisting militarism: security, subjectivity and subversion in contemporary movement*. Edinburgh: Edinburgh University Press.

Sabaratnam, M. (2017) *Decolonising intervention: international statebuilding in Mozambique*. London and New York: Rowman & Littlefield International.

Sahnoun, M. (2011) 'Interview with Mohamed Sahnoun', 30 July 2011, *Global Responsibility to Protect*, 3 (4), pp. 473–479.

Sangheri, J. (2016) 'Opening statement', Working Group on a United Nations Declaration on the Rights of Peasants and Other People Working in Rural Areas, Third Session, Geneva, 17 May 2016. Available at: www.ohchr.org/Documents/HRBodies/HRCouncil/WGPleasants/Session3/StatementsPresentations/Jyoti_Sanghera_OHCHR.doc (Accessed: 28 August 2016).

Seybolt, T. B. (2007) *Humanitarian military intervention: the conditions for success and failure*. Oxford: Oxford University Press.

Shawki, N. (2011) 'Responsibility to Protect: the evolution of an international norm', *Global Responsibility to Protect*, 3 (2), pp. 172–196.

Shiva, V. (2014) *The Vandana Shiva reader (culture of the land)*. Lexington, KY: University Press of Kentucky.

Simms, B. and Trim, D. J. B. (eds.) (2011) *Humanitarian intervention: a history*. Cambridge: Cambridge University Press.

Small Arms Survey (2015) 'Small arms survey 2015: weapons and the world'. Cambridge: Cambridge University Press. Available at: www.smallarmssurvey.org/publications/by-type/yearbook/small-arms-survey-2015.html (Accessed: 01 November 2017).

Souter, J. (2016) 'Good international citizenship and special responsibilities to protect refugees', *The British Journal of Politics and International Relations*, 18 (4), pp. 795–811.

Stavrianakis, A. (2016) 'Legitimizing liberal militarism: politics, law and war in the Arms Trade Treaty', *Third World Quarterly*, 37 (5), pp. 840–865.

Stavrianakis, A. and Selby, J. (eds.) (2012) *Militarism and international relations: political economy, security, theory*. London and New York: Routledge.

Stearman, K. (2011) 'UK arms sales to Libya – stop, start, stop and start again', *openDemocracy*, 06 December 2011. Available at: www.opendemocracy. net/kaye-stearman/uk-arms-sales-to-libya-stop-start-stop-and-start-again (Accessed: 17 August 2018).

Steinhoff, U. (2007) *The ethics of war and terrorism*. Oxford: Oxford University Press.

Suliman, M. (1997) 'Civil war in Sudan: the impact of ecological degradation', *Contributions in Black Studies*, 15, pp. 99–121.

Thakur, R. (2013) 'R2P after Libya and Syria: engaging emerging powers', *The Washington Quarterly*, 36 (2), pp. 61–76.

Theisen, O. M. (2008) 'Blood and soil? Resource scarcity and internal armed conflict revisited', *Journal of Peace Research*, 45 (6), pp. 801–818.

Tsikata, D. and Yaro, J. A. (2014) 'When a good business model is not enough: land transactions and gendered livelihood prospects in rural Ghana', *Feminist Economics*, 20 (1), pp. 202–226.

Twomey, H., Schiavoni, C. M., and Mongula, B. (2015) *Impacts of large-scale agricultural investments on small-scale farmers in the Southern Highlands of Tanzania: a right to food perspective*. Aachen: Misereor.

UCDP – Uppsala Conflict Data Program (2017) 'UCDP conflict encyclopedia', Department of Peace and Conflict Research, Uppsala University. Available at: www.ucdp.uu.se (Accessed: 03 August 2017).

UN – United Nations (2004) 'A more secure world: our shared responsibility', Report of the High-level Panel on Threats, Challenges and Change. New York: United Nations. Available at: www.un.org/ar/peacebuilding/pdf/ historical/hlp_more_secure_world.pdf (Accessed: 19 August, 2018).

UN – United Nations (2005) 'Resolution adopted by the General Assembly: 2005 World Summit Outcome', 24 October 2005, UN Doc A/RES/60/1, Geneva, United Nations. Available at: www.un.org/womenwatch/ods/A-RES-60-1-E. pdf (Accessed: 19 August 2018).

UN – United Nations (2009) 'Implementing the Responsibility to Protect', Report of the Secretary-General, 12 January 2009, UN Doc A/Res/63/677, Geneva, United Nations. Available at: http://undocs.org/A/RES/63/308 (Accessed: 19 August 2018).

UN – United Nations (2012a) 'Report of the Secretary-General's internal review panel on UN actions in Sri Lanka', November 2012. Available at: www. un.org/News/dh/infocus/Sri_Lanka/The_Internal_Review_Panel_report_on_ Sri_Lanka.pdf (Accessed: 19 August 2018).

UN – United Nations (2012b) 'The Responsibility to Protect: timely and decisive response', Report of the Secretary-General, 25 July 2012, UN Doc A/66/874–S/2012/578, Geneva, United Nations. Available at: http://undocs. org/A/66/874 (Accessed: 19 August 2018).

UN – United Nations (2014) 'Fulfilling our collective responsibility: international assistance and the Responsibility to Protect', Report of the Secretary-General, 11 July 2014, UN Doc A/68/947–S/2014/449, Geneva, United Nations. Available at: www.un.org/ga/search/view_doc.asp?symbol=A/68/947&referer=/ english/&Lang=E (Accessed: 19 August 2018).

UN – United Nations (2015a) 'A vital and enduring commitment: implementing the Responsibility to Protect', Report of the Secretary-General, 13 July 2015, UN Doc A/69/981-S/2015/500, Geneva, United Nations. Available at: https:// digitallibrary.un.org/record/798795/files/A_69_981-EN.pdf (Accessed: 19 August 2018).

UN – United Nations (2015b) 'Human cost of illicit flow of small arms, light weapons stressed in Security Council debate', 13 May 2015, SC/11889, Geneva, United Nations. Available at: www.un.org/press/en/2015/sc11889. doc.htm (Accessed: 19 August 2018).

UN – United Nations (2017) 'Implementing the Responsibility to Protect: accountability for prevention', Report of the Secretary-General, 10 August 2017, UN Doc A/71/1016–S/2017/556, Geneva, United Nations. Available at: http://undocs.org/S/2017/556 (Accessed: 19 August 2018).

UN Interagency Framework Team for Preventive Action (2012) 'Land and conflict'. Available at: www.un.org/en/events/environmentconflictday/pdf/ GN_Land_Consultation.pdf (Accessed: 19 August 2018).

UN News (2011) 'UN rights council recommends suspending Libya, orders inquiry into abuses', 25 February 2011. Available at: www.un.org/apps/news/story. asp?NewsID=37626#.WNEOPBSe9SU (Accessed: 19 August 2018).

UN News (2017) 'Yemen's "man-made catastrophe" is ravaging country, senior UN officials tell Security Council', 18 August 2017. Available at: www.un.org/ apps/news/story.asp?NewsID=57380#.WfnufBQo1od (Accessed: 19 August 2018).

UNSC – United Nations Security Council (2011) 'Resolution 1973 (2011)', 17 March 2011, S/RES/1973. Available at: www.un.org/en/ga/search/view_doc. asp?symbol=S/RES/1973(2011) (Accessed: 19 August 2018).

UNSC – United Nations Security Council (2013) 'Final report of the panel of experts established pursuant to Resolution 1973 (2011) concerning Libya', 09 March 2013, UN Doc S/2013/99. Available at: www.un.org/ga/search/ view_doc.asp?symbol=S/2013/99 (Accessed: 19 August 2018).

USCNS – US Commission on National Security/21st Century (2000) 'Seeking a national strategy: a concert for preserving security and promoting freedom', 15 April 2015. Available at: http://govinfo.library.unt.edu/nssg/PhaseII.pdf (Accessed: 27 June 2018).

van der Klaauw, J. (2015) 'Statement on Yemen', United Nations Office of the Humanitarian Coordinator for Yemen, 09 May 2015. Available at: https://reliefweb.int/sites/reliefweb.int/files/resources/HC%20Statement%20on%20Yemen%209%20May%202015.pdf (Accessed: 01 November 2017).

van Leeuwen, M. and van der Haar, G. (2016) 'Theorizing the land–violent conflict nexus', *World Development*, 78, pp. 94–104.

Vilmer, J. B. J. (2016) 'Ten myths about the 2011 intervention in Libya', *Washington Quarterly*, 39 (2), pp. 23–43.

Viotti, M. L. R (2011) 'Protection of civilians in armed conflicts', statement by H. E. Ambassador Maria Luiza Ribeiro Viotti, Permanent Representative of Brazil to the United Nations, 10 May 2011. Available at: http://responsibilitytoprotect.org/brazil.pdf (Accessed: 19 August 2018).

Vitoria, F. de (1991) 'On the American Indians', in Pagden, A. and Lawrance, J. (eds.) *Political Writings*. Cambridge: Cambridge University Press, pp. 231–292.

Vlassenroot, K. (ed.) (2013) 'Land issues and conflict in Eastern Congo: towards an integrated and participatory approach', Conflict Research Group, Available at: https://s3.amazonaws.com/ssrc-cdn1/crmuploads/new_publication_3/%7BD60A3932-A65A-E211-8EAC-001CC477EC84%7D.pdf (Accessed: 17 August 2018).

Waller, D. (1993) *Rwanda: which way now?* An Oxfam Country Profile. Oxford: Oxfam Professional Publisher.

Walling, C. B. (2015) 'Human rights norms, state sovereignty, and humanitarian intervention', *Human Rights Quarterly*, 37 (2), pp. 383–413.

Walzer, M. (2004) *Arguing about war.* New Haven, CT: Yale University Press.

Walzer, M. (2006) *Just and unjust wars: a moral argument with historical illustrations.* Revised ed. New York: Basic Books.

Walzer, M. (2011) 'The case against our attack on Libya', *The New Republic*, 20 March 2011. Available at: https://newrepublic.com/article/85509/the-case-against-our-attack-libya (Accessed: 17 August 2018).

Watson, C. (1991) *Exile from Rwanda: background to an invasion.* Washington, DC: U.S. Committee for Refugees.

Wearing, D. (2016) 'A shameful relationship: UK complicity in Saudi state violence', Campaign Against the Arms Trade, April 2016. Available at: www.caat.org.uk/campaigns/stop-arming-saudi/a-shameful-relationship.pdf (Accessed: 19 August 2018).

Weiss, T. G. (2004) 'The sunset of humanitarian intervention? The Responsibility to Protect in a unipolar era', *Security Dialogue*, 35 (2), pp. 135–153.

Wenar, L. (2016) *Blood oil: tyrants, violence, and the rules that run the world*. New York: Oxford University Press.

Wheeler, N. J. (2000) *Saving strangers: humanitarian intervention in international society*. Oxford: Oxford University Press.

Wheeler, N. J. and Dunne, T. (1998) 'Good international citizenship: a third war for British foreign policy', *International Affairs*, 74 (4), pp. 847–870.

WHO – World Health Organization (2015) 'Child mortality rates plunge by more than half since 1990 but global MDG target missed by wide margin: 16,000 children under 5 years old die each day', 09 September 2015. Available at: www.who.int/mediacentre/news/releases/2015/child-mortality-report/en/ (Accessed: 19 August 2018).

WHO – World Health Organization (2017a) '10 facts on the state of global health', May 2017. Available at: www.who.int/features/factfiles/global_burden/en/ (Accessed: 31 October 2017).

WHO – World Health Organization (2017b) 'World health statistics 2017: monitoring health for the SDGs, Sustainable Development Goals', Geneva: World Health Organization. Available at: www.who.int/gho/publications/ world_health_statistics/2017/en/ (Accessed: 19 August 2018).

WHO – World Health Organization (2018) 'Climate change and health', 01 February 2018. Available at: www.who.int/news-room/fact-sheets/detail/ climate-change-and-health (Accessed: 24 March 2018).

Whyte, J. (2017) '"Always on top"? The "Responsibility to Protect" and the persistence of colonialism', in Singh, J. G. and Kim, D. D. (eds.), *Postcolonial world*. London: Routledge, pp. 308–324.

Wibben, A. T. R. (2018) 'Why we need to study (US) militarism: a critical feminist lens', *Security Dialogue*, 49 (1/2), pp. 136–148.

Williams, P. D. (2011) 'The road to humanitarian war in Libya', *Global Responsibility to Protect*, 3 (2), pp. 248–259.

Wintour, P. (2016a) 'British MPs bear some blame for Aleppo tragedy, says George Osborne', *The Guardian*, 13 December 2016. Available at: www.theguardian. com/world/2016/dec/13/aleppo-syria-commons-debate-george-osborne (Accessed: 20 July 2018).

Wintour, P. (2016b) 'Ban Ki-moon adds to pressure on UK to stop arms sales to Saudis', *The Guardian*, 05 February 2016. Available at: www.theguardian. com/world/2016/feb/05/ban-ki-moon-yemen-war-uk-arms-sales-saudi-arabia (Accessed: 17 August 2018).

World Bank (2007) 'Agriculture for development: world development report 2008'. Washington, DC: World Bank. Available at: https://openknowledge.

worldbank.org/bitstream/handle/10986/5990/WDR%202008%20-%20
English.pdf?sequence=3&isAllowed=y (Accessed: 19 August 2018).

World Bank (2009) 'Awaking Africa's sleeping giants: prospects for commercial
agriculture in the Guinea Savannah zone and beyond'. Washington,
DC: World Bank. Available at: https://openknowledge.worldbank.org/
bitstream/handle/10986/2640/490460PUBoslee101OfficialoUseoOnly1.
pdf?sequence=1&isAllowed=y (Accessed: 19 August 2018).

World Bank (2016) 'Poverty and shared prosperity 2016: taking on inequality'.
Washington, DC: The World Bank. Available at: www.worldbank.org/en/
publication/poverty-and-shared-prosperity (Accessed: 19 August 2018).

INDEX

ZED

Zed is a platform for marginalised voices across the globe.

It is the world's largest publishing collective and a world leading example of alternative, non-hierarchical business practice.

It has no CEO, no MD and no bosses and is owned and managed by its workers who are all on equal pay.

It makes its content available in as many languages as possible.

It publishes content critical of oppressive power structures and regimes.

It publishes content that changes its readers' thinking.

It publishes content that other publishers won't and that the establishment finds threatening.

It has been subject to repeated acts of censorship by states and corporations.

It fights all forms of censorship.

It is financially and ideologically independent of any party, corporation, state or individual.

Its books are shared all over the world.

www.zedbooks.net
@ZedBooks